UNCONDITIONAL
FORGIVENESS

UNCONDITIONAL FORGIVENESS

Biblical Truth

or

Seedbed of Heresy?

A **Biblical** Examination of Forgiveness

James Szarszewski

LAMP OF TRUTH *Publishing*

ISBN 978-0-578-92685-8

Lamp of Truth Publishing

FOR

THOSE WHO HAVE EARS TO HEAR

CONTENTS

The only thing a sheep resolves by forgiving a wolf is the question of dinner plans . . . for the wolf!

PREFACE

I originally wrote the material in this book to be part of a larger work examining many different beliefs and teachings which have become prevalent in the church but which have no basis in Scripture. Many believers accept these doctrinal aberrations at face value without searching the Scriptures to see if they're actually true. The fact that these teachings are so frequently taught and so readily believed by so many in the church is troubling to say the least.

Then, upon hearing some of these same teachings while in seminary some years ago, I went from being troubled to downright burdened. Especially since the Bible was being used to "support" these doctrines. Grieved at hearing the word of God so perverted, I spent much time in prayer and the earnest study of Scripture. I felt the Lord urging me to write what I was learning, to examine these teachings in the bright light of His word for the benefit of others.

The work, however, quickly grew and was fast becoming a tome, which I had not anticipated. To do justice to the various topics caused *chapters* to grow into *sections*. Some sections grew large enough to become books in themselves.

The book dragged on through the ebb and flow of life. Then one day I had an epiphany (better late than never!) that perhaps it would be better if *all* the subjects were treated as stand-alone books. This would certainly make the work less daunting to readers, who could simply select the subject of greatest interest to them. And it would definitely help *me* to have something to show for a book, the writing of which seemed to be endless!

It is my sincere hope that this work will enlighten, encourage, and feed hungry saints . . . and wake up sleeping ones. I write with great concern for the church, for genuine believers who truly want to know God and walk in His word.

Some may think I overreact, and accuse me of upsetting the apple cart or rocking the boat without warrant. I disagree, for reasons which will soon become apparent. Sometimes the apple cart *needs* to be upset, especially if rotten apples are being peddled as good and wholesome. Sometimes the boat *needs* to be rocked, especially when heading for the falls and those aboard are asleep. Sometimes the boat, if irretrievably unsound and unsafe, should be sunk.

Some may also think me too severe, even harsh at times. I can only say that this is not my heart. And indeed I may, with Luther, share this failing. It may be an unavoidable consequence of loving the truth and hating error. I am not so naive as to think the things I write can be said no other way. I am human after all, and I pray that my mode of expression will in no way obscure the truth that desperately needs to be heard.

I confess, it is not my custom to sugarcoat things. And if there's one thing I've learned, it's that people *do like their sugar*. I am well aware that the truth in the following pages may not be readily embraced by all. It may even be vigorously opposed by some.

Not everyone has a heart for truth. Our Lord made that abundantly clear. His familiar refrain, "He who has ears to hear, let him hear" provides a concise sampling of His audience. And since "a disciple is not above his teacher," I shall not presume to aim any higher.

If you are committed to protecting and maintaining your biases, this book will not help you.

I write for the benefit of those who are teachable. Those who can still be persuaded by a clear presentation of biblical truth—even if you have never seriously considered the things you're about to read.

Jesus said the truth will make you free, a reference we all know well. But we rarely consider the opposite. If the truth makes us free then anything that is not truth brings us into bondage.

Understanding this will snuff out indifference and ignite within us a passion for truth. It will also ignite an equally passionate hatred for lies; it's the flip side of the same coin. The psalmist knew this. He declared, "From Your precepts I get understanding; therefore *I hate every false way*" (Psalm 119.104).

Our beliefs have consequences. It is not merely *believing*, but *what* we believe, that is vital. Our beliefs bear fruit in our lives, good and bad. There is no inherent virtue in faith itself, even sincere faith. People believe a great many things, often quite sincerely, especially when it comes to religion. It's been said that sincerely believing a lie means only that you're sincerely deceived.

There was a time not that long ago when the brightest minds in the world sincerely believed the world was flat, and that if you sailed far enough, you would fall off the edge. Their sincerity had no bearing on the correctness of their (erroneous) belief.

Moreover, just because certain beliefs are shared by the masses does not make them true. This is a poor and perilous method of authenticity, inasmuch as truth is never sipped from the chalice of popular opinion. While deception, on the other hand, thrives on numbers. The more a lie is believed, the stronger it becomes, and we confirm our delusions in one another.

We should not fear an honest scrutiny of our beliefs. Those that are *not* true, we retain to our own hurt. Those that are become even stronger after investigation. It is error that fears the examination table, for it is disguised as truth. Careful analysis reveals that it's a lie. Yet, however closely you examine truth, it can never be found to be anything other than what it is—*truth!*

I am resolved not to litter this work with extra-biblical "references." Therefore, footnotes will be kept to a minimum save for explanatory notes, clarifying comments, and the like. The bloat of references is a favored tack in much of academia but is especially odious to me. In my opinion, appealing to a myriad of scholars, theologians, and other so-called spiritual authorities to "prove" something against the teaching of Scripture is a colossal waste of time.

My conscience is wed to Scripture alone, and I hope yours is too. Thus, I have no desire to drag you through a swampland of dubious scholastic references reflecting a consensus that has strayed from biblical truth.

I am still simple-minded enough to believe that Scripture should be our highest authority. Therefore, I will endeavor to examine this subject by the Scriptures and plain reason. In truth, if *that* is not enough, then it really *doesn't matter who I cite!* If you cannot be persuaded by the word of God, appealing to other sources is pointless.

Unconditional forgiveness is arguably the most pervasive of all the topics in the original collection, so it was a fairly easy decision to start here. I humbly submit this the first book. My earnest prayer is that it brings you into greater peace and freedom, which the clear truth of God's word always will do.

INTRODUCTION

A Bizarre Deviation

One day, purely for my own organizational benefit, I decided to compile in my journal a list of the false teachings and beliefs I had been encountering with increasing frequency among those professing to be followers of Christ. When I came to forgiveness, I paused to ponder what I should call it, for I had not, up to that point, known quite what to call this teaching.

"Unconditional Forgiveness" seemed to describe it most aptly, I thought, so I scribbled that in my journal and continued my list. I was still in seminary at the time, so you can imagine my shock when *just a few days later* the professor in my New Testament class was attempting to defend this doctrine. I had heard this teaching many times in many different places, and I found myself thinking, "Not again! Not *here too!*"

The real shock, however, came when he

actually called it "unconditional forgiveness," and pompously declared it a *biblical* doctrine! I had never heard that term *anywhere!* But the fact that I had just entered it into my journal as a false doctrine and was now hearing this professor make such a pontifical "decree"—using the *exact designation* I wrote in my journal!—that sent a chill up my spine. How's that for getting your attention?!

Experiences like this sent me to my knees, fervently praying about this subject to be sure I was hearing the Lord correctly. Again and again, He reaffirmed the truths He had shown me and urged me to write what I saw.

Now let me be crystal clear. I strongly believe in forgiveness. I believe it's a biblical doctrine, and one that every believer must walk in. But I have yet to hear a truly balanced biblical teaching on the subject. I have yet to hear it presented in a manner consistent with what the Scriptures actually teach. Every time I hear a teaching on forgiveness I listen intently, hoping to hear a sound biblical treatment, but walk away deeply grieved, for God's word is egregiously mishandled and its truth trampled into an unrecognizable heap.

Daring to question it seems to make one extremely controversial. Many I have spoken with simply do not have ears to hear. They refuse to hear anything other than the usual treatment of this doctrine (which I'll delineate in a moment).

It's been said that the greatest lie is the one closest to the truth. This one is a *diabolical masterpiece!* Yet I firmly believe the Lord is able to open the eyes of all who truly *want to see* and *know*

His truth. Otherwise, I write in vain.

Many have never questioned what is usually taught on forgiveness. You've had unconditional forgiveness hammered into your heads so often that any attempt to challenge what you've heard sounds an alarm in your soul.

Consequently, you may be tempted to think me a raving lunatic. But I urge you to read on with an open heart, listening intently for the voice of the Holy Spirit. I assure you, I want nothing but His truth. And I remain convinced that an intelligent, unbiased reading of Scripture can clear away the smoke that clouds the standard teaching on forgiveness.

A. W. Tozer said the sacred duty of all Christians is to be certain that their beliefs correspond exactly to truth. We should make it our solemn practice to measure *every* doctrine against the sound teaching of Scripture, shedding every contrary belief.

Vague ideas and false notions about forgiveness abound, particularly where forgiving others is concerned. How many times have you or someone you know been wronged by someone in the church, only to hear others glibly advise, "Well, you *have* to forgive 'em."

Pastors and other leaders in the church are frightfully quick to respond by urging those who have been sinned against to forgive the offender—as if forgiveness were merely a one-sided transaction having nothing to do with the offender.

Forgiveness is often hailed as the "be all and end all," imbued with mystical power and touted as the supreme spiritual path to true freedom, peace, and joy. It's a stock favorite among those in the counseling professions.

I know seminary professors who have adopted it as their own doctrinal hobby horse. I've had the unenviable experience of being part of their "captive" audience. It's been downright excruciating to hear them prattle on about forgiveness with a mishmash of cheap psychology, schmaltzy stories, and mutilated Scriptures.

Bookstores and libraries are teeming with titles on forgiveness, yet most are mere psycho-babble, new age folderol, and religious sentimentalism. As such, they offer no benefit to the sincere believer seeking to know what the Bible teaches about forgiveness.

In a nutshell, this teaching (at least from those claiming a Christian perspective) goes something like this: We must forgive any and all offenders for all offenses, *without regard to the offender's attitude(!)*, because that is what God *commands* us to do; because *that* is the right and Christian response to the sins of others (and some will add, "because that is how God forgives us for our sins").

And the striking consensus is that this *is biblical!* It is preached with passion, taught with conviction, and believed most ardently. Like counterfeit money, it has been circulated so widely and with such fervor, that who can now determine the extent of its reach?

There are many problems with this doctrine and we'll explore each of these more fully in the pages ahead.

> ➤ It is not biblically sound
> ➤ It denies reality and encourages denial
> ➤ It sets up a false dichotomy
> ➤ It psychologizes the truth of Scripture
> ➤ It does not effect reconciliation
> ➤ It destroys the standard of truth and righteousness
> ➤ It trivializes the destructive nature of sin.

Beyond this, however, this teaching embodies a gross fallacy and distorts not only the Bible but *the very nature and character of God.*

I heard a wise preacher once say that when a half-truth is presented as the whole-truth, it becomes an *un-truth.* The usual teaching on forgiveness represents only a half-truth—*at best.*

Tremendous pressure is placed on the person sinned against to dole out forgiveness *indiscriminately* with precious little mention *(or none at all!)* of the offender and the requisite *condition* of forgiveness.

This doctrine eliminates the necessity of repentance. But is this what the Bible really teaches? And if repentance is truly unnecessary, what are the implications of this doctrine? Let's find out.

Chapter 1

SLOPPY EXEGESIS

It is foolish and irresponsible to read our own ideas into a passage of Scripture (a practice known as *eisegesis*) rather than letting the text speak, and drawing from it what it actually says *(exegesis)*.

It is also a very unwise interpretive practice to put undue emphasis on one isolated passage when Scripture speaks elsewhere on the subject, and thereby neglect the whole counsel of the word of God.

The interpretations and conclusions of the proponents of unconditional forgiveness stray on both counts. For while they take verses from the Bible they believe supports their position (those who at least appeal to the Bible), they do so in a way that actually contradicts the teaching of Scripture. Therefore, we must examine these passages carefully if we are to learn the truth as God intended.

THE LORD'S TEACHING ON FORGIVENESS

In what is commonly referred to as the Lord's prayer, Jesus instructed His disciples to pray, "And forgive us our debts, as we also have forgiven our debtors." Then He continued, "For if you forgive men for their transgressions, your heavenly Father will also forgive you. But if you do not forgive men, then your Father will not forgive your transgressions" (Matthew 6:12, 14, 15).

There are those who imagine (and fervently preach) that Jesus was here teaching that we must dispense an unconditional, automatic forgiveness. This interpretation indeed comes from their own imagination, for it must be *read into* the text (*eisegesis*).

If anything should be assumed about this passage, it is *the repentance* of those who sin against us, for as we'll see in a moment, Jesus makes it abundantly clear elsewhere in His teaching that repentance is the fundamental, indispensable, and unwavering condition of forgiveness.

But first, does it not strike you as extremely inconsistent that our Lord would teach us to pray and ask our Father for forgiveness when we sin against Him—making it an intentional, daily part of our praying—yet instruct *us* to forgive automatically without a similar entreaty from those who sin against us?

This passage *might* be somewhat ambiguous *if* it was the only passage in the Bible about forgiveness. But it is *not* the only passage. The Lord's teaching is crystal clear elsewhere on the subject. We must never interpret one passage of Scripture in a way that clearly contradicts other passages.

I actually heard a seminary professor once say (as if to avoid other "complications" in Scripture and their obvious implications to this doctrine) that there was no need to appeal to *other* passages about forgiveness because the Lord had already laid down the guidelines for forgiveness right here in Matthew 6.

What logic! *This* is the ministry "training" I paid absurd amounts of money *for?!* There is simply no (good) reason to treat this passage as if it were the only word on the subject, and flatly ignore the rest of Scripture.

Our Lord amply expands and elaborates His teaching on forgiveness cogently in Matthew 18 (and elsewhere). And if we are His followers we must accept and obey all of His teaching.

Imposing our own sentimentalized ideas about forgiveness onto Matthew 6, and stopping there, is hyper moronity. In fairness, not everyone does this. Some appeal to other passages they believe support unconditional forgiveness. But they do so with the same sloppy exegesis demonstrated here. Their biases keep them from seeing the truth in the passages they profess to understand. The result is that they do not actually teach what *the Bible teaches* at all but spout only half-truths and error.

THE PARABLE OF
THE UNFORGIVING SERVANT

It is astonishing that many appeal to the parable of the unforgiving servant to "prove" unconditional forgiveness! Because far from *supporting* this doctrine, this parable actually *obliterates* it! Isn't that just like the enemy to take a clear teaching of Scripture and completely invert it?

It is more than ironic that the advocates of unconditional forgiveness use this text (Matthew 18:21-35) to support their doctrine (emphasizing the judgment on unforgiveness), for their exposition is so horribly deficient that it forces me to wonder how they can understand *any* passage of Scripture.

Let's look at the passage and see if their doctrinal card castle can stand when we open the window of honest interpretation.

> 21 Then Peter came and said to Him, "Lord, how often shall my brother sin against me and I forgive him? Up to seven times?"
> 22 Jesus said to him, "I do not say to you, up to seven times, but up to seventy times seven.
> 23 "For this reason the kingdom of heaven may be compared to a certain king who wished to settle accounts with his slaves.
> 24 "And when he had begun to settle them, there was brought to him one who owed him ten thousand talents.[1]
> 25 "But since he did not have the means to repay, his lord commanded him to be sold, along with his wife and children and all that he had, and repayment to be made.

---

1   About $10,000,000 in silver content. One talent was equivalent to more than fifteen years of a laborer's wages. This means the debt was impossible to repay.

26 "So the slave fell to the ground and prostrated himself before him, saying, 'Have patience with me and I will repay you everything.'

27 "And the lord of that slave felt compassion and released him and forgave him the debt.

28 "But that slave went out and found one of his fellow slaves who owed him a hundred denarii;[2] and he seized him and began to choke him, saying, 'Pay back what you owe.'

29 "So his fellow slave fell down and began to entreat him, saying, 'Have patience with me and I will repay you.'

30 "But he was unwilling and went and threw him in prison until he should pay back what was owed.

31 "So when his fellow slaves saw what had happened, they were deeply grieved and came and reported to their lord all that had happened.

32 "Then summoning him, his lord said to him, 'You wicked slave, I forgave you all that debt because you entreated me.

33 'Should you not also have had mercy on your fellow slave, even as I had mercy on you?'

34 "And his lord, moved with anger, handed him over to the torturers until he should repay all that was owed him.

35 "So shall My heavenly Father also do to you, if each of you does not forgive his brother from your heart."

I shall not exegete every nuance of this passage, but what I wish to point out is an egregious omission every time I hear this taught, which then slaughters the whole point of the parable. What makes this passage so potent, of course, is how Jesus *compares* the attitudes and actions of the first slave to the second. (I do not get much argument here.)

But what is consistently overlooked (or flatly ignored) is the way they're *exactly the same!* I am

---

2   The denarius was the daily wage of a laborer. So, this would have amounted to just over four month's wages, a paltry amount compared to the first slave.

positively mystified as to how one can possibly miss the fact that they **both repented!** When confronted, they **both** acknowledge their guilt, prostrate themselves and plead, "Have patience with me, and I will repay you." The first slave was forgiven a large debt because he fell down and begged the king for mercy, but when his fellow slave, who owed far less, *displayed the very same contrition*, the first slave refused.

This puts the passage in an entirely new light. If this parable were rightly taught, and repentance put back into the usual teaching on forgiveness, I would have no problem with it.

When we confront a brother and he humbles himself and repents, if *in the face of his repentance* and willingness to make amends, we stubbornly *refuse* to forgive him, then there's a problem. *That* is the evil Jesus is warning against here! *That* is what makes unforgiveness so evil. But this is not how this parable is generally taught.

It is greatly concerning that of all the preachers and professors I have heard teach out of this passage, **not one** of them mentioned this utterly essential part of the parable. Jesus is **not** teaching an automatic, unconditional forgiveness here. He highlights the disparity between God forgiving us so much *when we repent* and us not forgiving others *when they repent*, but **repentance is the constant**.

Jesus is underscoring the evil of someone hardening their heart and *refusing* to forgive *in the face of a brother's repentance!* I don't know if this should be called *delusional creativity* or what, for I am absolutely astounded that anyone in their right mind can read this passage and actually think that it teaches unconditional forgiveness! O how the pristine waters of truth have been muddied!

Even more astonishing and shedding even more light on this parable is the fact that Jesus had just given His disciples *very explicit instructions* on what to do when a brother sins against us—especially when he refuses to repent.

> If your brother sins against you,[3] go and reprove him in private; if he listens to you, you have won your brother. But if he does not listen to you, take one or two more with you, so that by the mouth of two or three witnesses every word may be confirmed. And if he refuses to listen to them, tell it to the church; and if he refuses to listen even to the church, let him be to you as a Gentile and a tax-gatherer [i.e. an unbeliever] (Matthew 18:15-17).

The Lord provided us a *patently clear procedure* in the case of an unrepentant offender, and forgiving him anyway *appears nowhere in His instructions!*

We are not simply to ignore sin and dispense indiscriminate forgiveness on those who do not repent. We are to confront them with an eye toward restoration—which *cannot happen without repentance.* Jesus gave us specific steps to follow to bring about a brother's repentance—and forgiveness

---

3 Some early mss do not contain the words *against you.* However, they are implied from the context. On one hand, if a brother sins, it certainly includes his sinning *against you.* Beyond this, Peter's reply (v. 21) to the Lord's procedure here reveals that this is clearly the sense. Luke follows the same pattern (Lk. 17:3, 4).

is *not* one of them...*unless he repents!*

In the case of those who refuse to repent, you will not find anywhere in Scripture where we are commanded to *forgive them anyway!* This would totally undermine the Lord's teaching here. His teaching culminates with the brother ultimately being put out of the church and regarded a pagan—specifically because he would not repent. In his steadfast refusal to repent, he shows himself to be unamenable to the truth and unwilling to renounce his sin. Jesus, in effect, is saying, "This does not characterize one of *My* disciples!" And He was teaching us that forgiveness *cannot occur* until this essential condition is met.

This passage completely breaks down and makes absolutely no sense if we overlay it with our milquetoast "forgive no matter what" brand of forgiveness, which essentially puts the onus on *the one sinned against* rather than where Jesus said it rightfully belongs!

Chapter 2

HOW DOES GOD FORGIVE US?

I readily concede that the title of this chapter seems like a ridiculous question to ask. But given the dense spiritual fog shrouding this subject I suppose it is not altogether surprising that we must address it.

It appears the advocates of unconditional forgiveness believe God forgives us automatically and without condition. For, in an effort to buttress their position, some appeal to a couple of Bible verses that compare how we forgive *one another* to how the Lord forgives *us*. Their reasoning, of course, is flawed, but let us look at the verses and you can see for yourself.

> Be kind to one another, tender-hearted, forgiving each other, just as God in Christ also has forgiven you (Ephesians 4:32).

> ...bearing with one another, and forgiving each other, whoever has a complaint against anyone; just as the Lord forgave you, so also should you (Colossians 3:13).

Those I've heard cite these verses just *read* them and then stop, with an air of triumph, as if no explanation is needed, and the "truth" they are attempting to prove is self-evident. I have listened to them in utter bewilderment, waiting for some attempt, some expository effort to connect these verses to unconditional forgiveness, thinking, "*Well...?! Go on!*" But, alas, no explanation is given.

Therefore, the only "proof," as preposterous as it sounds, is the assumption that we are forgiven unconditionally by God. However, these passages do not remotely support this "interpretation." In fact, they teach the exact opposite.

It is clear that Paul's exhortations for us to forgive one another are modeled on how we were forgiven by God. This is no great feat of interpretation. The words "just as" are comparative words. We are to forgive one another *just as* or *in the same way* God forgives us.

This they themselves observe but their bias then wrests an altogether different interpretation from the text. (It's almost as if the Holy Spirit anticipated this distortion and, to avoid any possible ambiguity, inspired Paul to pen the words "just as" specifically to qualify "forgiving each other.")

So it begs the question, "How does God forgive *us*?" Whether initially, at the point of salvation, or any time thereafter, the answer is the same and requires no lengthy deliberation.

But let me pose the question another way, simplifying so that it requires only a yes or no answer. Can anyone get into the kingdom of God without repentance? Can anyone be saved without repentance? Do you believe that when you sin, it really doesn't matter whether you repent because God forgives you automatically? When you harden your heart and choose to walk in sin, stubbornly refusing to repent, does God forgive you anyway?

If you answered "yes" to *any* of these, then I'm afraid you don't understand the gospel at all, and are not even walking with God. In fact, you have not been born again and remain outside the kingdom of God, for without repentance you have never gained entrance (Luke 13:1-5).

We will discuss repentance more in the next chapter but, in order to remove any and all confusion, allow me to share with you how God forgives us.

Remember that Jesus Himself taught us in the Lord's prayer to make petitions for forgiveness a normal, daily part of our praying. If we're forgiven unconditionally, why is this necessary? Would it not make the Lord's instructions meaningless, a mere empty religious exercise? (That is *never* our Lord's objective! He openly and consistently condemned pretense and religiosity).

Remember also the parable of the unforgiving slave. When the king summoned the slave to confront him, the king reminded him, "I forgave you all that debt" (what was his reason?) *"because you entreated me*. Should you not *also* have had mercy on your fellow slave, *even as*" (note again these comparative words) "I had mercy on you?"

How did the king have mercy on the slave? By forgiving him *when* he cried out for mercy and promised to repay. The slave clearly demonstrated a heart of repentance. The inference is clear—if the slave had not entreated him, he would not have been forgiven.

The prodigal son is also a moving example of repentance. He came to his senses, got up and returned with a contrite heart, confessing his sins. "Father, I have sinned against heaven and in your sight; I am no longer worthy to be called your son" (Luke 15:21). Had he not done that, he would not have been received, forgiven and restored by his father. It's that simple.

In fact, upon the son's return home, the words of his father sum it up plainly, "...this son of mine *was* dead, and has come to life again; he *was* lost, and has been found" (Luke 15:24). The difference between death and life, lost and found? Repentance.

David declared, "You, Lord, are good, and ready to forgive, and abundant in mercy to all who call upon You" (Psalm 86:5). Notice, God is *ready* to forgive. Being *ready* to do something is not the same as *doing* it. If I'm *ready* to eat, I am *not* eating. No one says, "I am ready to eat" if he is presently eating or has just finished a meal.

Being ready speaks of being disposed or prepared for some action, not already engaged in that action. If troops are ready for battle, they are not currently fighting. God is *ready* to forgive...so why doesn't He just forgive? (This creates a problem for those teaching unconditional forgiveness.)

The phrase is anticipatory. "Ready" implies that God is waiting for something (or else He would just go ahead and forgive). But what is He waiting for? *Us!* The context reveals that He's waiting for us to *repent!* Look at the next phrase...He is "abundant in mercy to *all who call upon Him*" (a specific group who perform a specific action).

The context of the verse is forgiveness. God is good and ready to forgive. When we call upon Him, He has mercy on us and forgives us. His mercy is not so dispensed to those who do not call upon Him.

The apostle John turns the lens to an even sharper focus. In a verse every Christian should memorize, John declares, "If we confess our sins, He is faithful and just to forgive us our sins and to cleanse us from all unrighteousness" (1 John 1:9). If. *If!*

Legend has it that the ancient king of Macedonia and father of Alexander the Great, Philip II, who conquered and renamed the city Philippi after himself, sent a message to Sparta saying "If I enter Laconia, I will level Sparta to the ground." The Spartans sent back a terse reply with only a single word: "If."

By its very definition, "if" is a highly conditional word. It signifies a condition on which something depends. "If" is one of the most important words in the Bible. It means: "*if* and *only if* and never *not if* some action is performed by God, myself, or others." In this case, *we* perform the action, upon which hangs the divine response. *If* we confess our sins, God will forgive us. If we do not, He will not. Can it be any clearer?

The assertion that God forgives us unconditionally is monstrous! The whole weight of Scripture decries such an obvious absurdity. We have clearly seen by the Scriptures that God does *not* forgive us unconditionally. He requires something from us and that something is repentance. That is our part, and He will not do our part.

Now if God will not forgive us unless we repent, it is unthinkable that He would expect us to forgive one another without the very same condition. Thus, the verses above, where Paul exhorts us to forgive one another *just as* God forgave us, not only fail to support the doctrine of unconditional forgiveness but diametrically oppose it.

How do I know this? Well, if Paul is actually teaching us to forgive without repentance, then he doesn't follow his own teaching. He convicts himself of hypocrisy and cannot be taken seriously.

He rebuked the church at Corinth for tolerating the sinner in their midst, urging them to deal with him and excommunicate him if need be (see 1 Corinthians 5). If the interpretation of the blind guides is correct, why would Paul rebuke the church? Would he not have urged a wholesale forgiveness instead?

Paul later writes the Corinthians that he is ready to visit them for the third time but says he is afraid he may have to deal with them harshly because many of them have sinned in the past and have not yet repented (see 2 Corinthians 12:20, 21). That seems decidedly inconsistent if Paul believes we should just forgive unconditionally.

How about the agitators in the churches of Galatia, who were telling believers they needed to be circumcised in order to be saved. Paul wrote these believers a very pointed letter saying if anyone preaches a different gospel, *let him be accursed* (Galatians 1:9). He told them, "the one who is disturbing you will *bear his judgment*" (Galatians 5:10). Then, in an obvious tone of righteous anger, he said, "I wish that those who are troubling you would not just stop at circumcision. I wish they would go all the way *and emasculate themselves!*" (Galatians 5:12). Whoa! Watch out, Paul! Sounds like you might have a root of bitterness![4]

In another instance, Paul urged his young delegate, Timothy, to rebuke the sinning elders at Ephesus publicly so that the others would take warning (1 Timothy 5:20). Should he not rather have urged Timothy to forgive them?!

Finally, he warned Timothy about the apostate, Alexander, who "did me much harm" (2 Timothy 4:14). Paul wrote, "The Lord will repay him for what he has done." Come on, Paul! Make up your mind. You said we're supposed to forgive him!

So you can see, Paul's teaching in the verses at the beginning of this chapter cannot be "interpreted" in a way that advocates an unconditional forgiveness. Paul would chafe at the twisting of his words.

Moreover, this "interpretation" is an affront to the crystal clear teaching of our Lord Jesus Christ. As to how our Lord taught us to forgive one another,

4   This is a common scare tactic used by those who teach unconditional forgiveness. I discuss this fully in chapter 7.

let me give you one more passage to show you just how clear He made this. He did not leave it up to our own muddled imagination. Some things in Scripture may be unclear. This is *not* one of them.

We have discussed the folly of stopping at one verse when Scripture speaks elsewhere on the subject. We must submit ourselves to the whole counsel of God. We looked at the parable of the unforgiving servant in the last chapter. If from that parable it remains in any way unclear that repentance is an essential condition of forgiveness, believe it or not, it gets even clearer.

In a parallel passage from Luke's gospel, Jesus expands and clarifies the answer to Peter's question about forgiving his brother. He leaves no possible room for confusion or misinterpretation.

After warning His disciples about stumbling blocks, Jesus said to them, "Be on your guard! (Lit., Take heed to yourselves). If your brother [or sister] sins against you, rebuke him; and **if** [*there's that pesky word again!*] **he repents**, forgive him. And if he sins against you seven times in a day, **and returns to you seven times, saying, 'I repent,'** forgive him" (Luke 17:3, 4). The Lord's teaching here needs no clarification.

The proponents of unconditional forgiveness deftly avoid this passage. Our Lord's teaching is so simple, so conclusive, and *so devastating to their position.*

This could not be any more straightforward. Even a child can grasp this. Our Lord is not speaking in riddles. He does not mince words. This is not a difficult concept.

The Lord's teaching here and in Matthew 18:15-17 is abundantly clear. You have the Lord's instructions and you have those who teach that you should forgive *without* following the Lord's instructions. They cannot both be right! The question is, who will you obey?

Chapter 3

REPENTANCE:

The Lost Doctrine In The Church

Shortly after I started writing this book, I happened upon an article about forgiveness in a renewal magazine, written by an evangelical seminary professor. To say the article was disappointing would be a triumph in understatement. The article was called, *The Realities of Forgiveness,* but it should have been called, *The Absurdities of Forgiveness*, at least the forgiveness he described.[5]

---

5   This appeared in an issue of Good News Magazine somewhere around 2008 but I could not find the exact date. The writer of the article was Kenneth Collins. I'm sure I retained a copy of this issue for reference but (years later) was unable to locate it. I was surprised that an internet search produced no results. It's just as well. If I had written such an abysmal article that did not reflect the teaching of Scripture, I should be very happy if no one could find it.

This article is a striking example of the pap being fed to the sheep. This is not meant to be an *ad hominem* response in any way and I do not wish to spend much time on this. I simply want to point out a few of the more egregious errors and absurdities in the article, to illustrate just how far the church has strayed in its understanding of forgiveness—because teaching like this *keeps perpetuating the lies!*

The writer asserts, "It is Christianity alone among world religions that places forgiveness at the very heart of the faith in its proclamation that Christ died for the forgiveness of sins of the whole world."

This struck me as an odd twist of a scriptural phrase. John said that Jesus is the propitiation (satisfaction) for the sins of the whole world (1 John 2:2). This means that the Lord's atoning sacrifice, the payment for the sins of the whole world has been made, but it most assuredly does *not* mean that the sins of the whole world are thus automatically forgiven. Therefore, I concede that Christ died *for the sins* of the whole world, but not *for the forgiveness of sins* of the whole world, which is dangerously close to heresy (and which I am sure this writer did not intend).

If Christ died for *the forgiveness* of sins of the whole world, that means the whole world is forgiven. And if the whole world is forgiven, then the whole world is (or will be) saved...and this we shall revisit later. As for the Christian proclamation, what Jesus actually said was, "that **repentance** for forgiveness of sins should be proclaimed in His name..." (Luke 24:47). Is it not alarming how this vitally important word could be conspicuously omitted in an

40

evangelical professor's epitome of the proclamation of the faith?

Later, this professor cites another professor who avows, "Christianity is a religion in which sinners have all the advantages...they can talk about you every time you leave the room, and *it is your job to excuse them* with no thought of getting even. *The burden is on you*" (emphasis mine). From the context of the article where this quote appeared, "sinners" represent those in the church, in which case I must vehemently disagree.

Is this not gossip, slander, and backbiting? And are these not still sins? I don't know what kind of Bible this person has, or what kind of church home, but I want no part of it. This is an appalling expression of apathy and stupidity. While I am certainly not condoning revenge, Scripture does not say "our job" is to excuse them and ignore sin, *but to confront them* and *deal with* sin (as our Lord instructed us). The burden then is clearly *on the sinner* to repent.

Further touting the merits of unconditional forgiveness, this professor then advocates a bizarre regimen of reframing and emotional casuistry as a pathway to peace, finding sanction for this regimen "according to some researchers" and because "several studies have shown."

He writes, "A common theme in the contemporary literature on forgiveness [you see where he is basing his theology] reveals that those who have come to a sense of peace...have done so *through a change in attitude, viewing both the perpetrator **and the evil itself** in new ways*" (italics and bold emphasis mine). He then cites a pastor who "maintains that forgiveness entails an 'intentional decision to *change how we feel about what happened and what it means to us*'" (emphasis mine). And so goes this "theme." As you can see, the absurdities are rife. When we set aside the wisdom of Scripture, this is the folly that replaces it.

Viewing the perpetrator and the evil in new ways and changing how we feel about it *never deals with the problem*. And it helps no one. It negates the truth, encourages denial, and demonstrates an odious passivity—all part and parcel of a saltless, sapless, toothless Christianity currently peddled to the world.

Scripture never tells us to look at sin differently. This is a big part of the problem with today's church. We are to see sin exactly as it is, in all its horrible ugliness, and then *deal with it*. Instructing people to look at sin differently sounds utterly ridiculous in light of the clear scriptural teaching to confront and rebuke the sinner for his sin. And if need be, if he refuses to repent, to "Remove the wicked man from among yourselves" (1 Corinthians 5:13; Matthew 18:15-17).

At one point, this professor seems like he begins to acknowledge the seriousness of sin. He speaks of holy love and glib forgiveness appearing cheap. I thought, "Okay, perhaps he will return now from his holiday from biblical truth and reason." But alas, all we are given is more of the same.

He quickly quells his concerns about a glib forgiveness by appealing to a "theologian," who calls for a strange and further mutilated forgiveness:

"What is needed then, is a kind of forgiveness that is able to say, 'It *does* matter terribly. It will never be all right. But I still forgive you.'"

But I still forgive you?! Where is he finding these people? Obviously this pious piffle is uttered to an unrepentant perpetrator, and, as we discussed above, this flies in the face of the crystal clear teaching of the word of God. This is psycho-babble at its best.

Scripture nowhere commands us, in the face of an unrepentant brother or sister, merely to *forgive them anyway*. This epitomizes what is currently being taught. Yet, it is the teaching of man, not God. And it came from the pit. This professor can cite people till the cows come home... and the pigs come home (and even the chickens and the rats and the fleas on their backs!), but it will not change one word of Holy Scripture—for those who have ears to hear and a heart to obey. All right, one more example from this article is all I can bear.

This professor cites yet another professor who pontificates, "At bottom, forgiveness *cannot* be grounded in justice *or repentance*" (emphasis mine). Did you *hear* that?! Can you *believe* this?! At bottom of what? The barrel of his own benighted bias where he is scraping this drivel? If there is no repentance then what exactly *are* we forgiving?

Forgiveness is a response to something, and that something is repentance. Trying to forgive where there is no repentance is like trying to digest food you have not eaten.

Then, hoping to drive home his point, he continues, "In fact, the clear majority of texts about forgiveness from the early church fathers *do not mention repentance*" (emphasis mine).

Oh!...the church *fathers*...Well, doesn't that just change everything? Excuse me while I trade in my Bible for the writings of *the church fathers!* What about *what God says?!*

The professor who penned this article referenced Scripture all of twice, and after forcing it through the meat grinder of unconditional forgiveness, its truth was unrecognizable. Then he appealed to no less than 12 (I stopped counting here) extra-biblical sources (as if this bilge is supposed to hold some sway over my conscience).

The plethora of his sources "proved" absolutely nothing, except the fact that they clearly *do not understand* biblical forgiveness. I dare say, if these be the "experts," the church is in big trouble!

> "O My people! Those who guide you lead
> you astray, and confuse the direction of
> your paths" (Isaiah 3:12).

This is a classic example of the blind leading...the blind. And we'll remain blind until we start testing all things by the word of God and refuse to follow blind guides.

I don't give a papal tiara what the early church fathers (or anyone else, come to that) wrote, if it conflicts with Holy Scripture! Yea, let God be true though every man a liar! Let us cry out with the Psalmist: "O Lord, 'I consider all Your precepts concerning all things to be right; I hate every false way!'" (Psalm 119:128).

Are you not weary of hearing people prattle

on endlessly, appealing to just about everyone and everything under the sun *except Scripture?!* It's like the Bible is no longer enough. Our (higher?) learning has engendered an arrogance that has secretly seduced us into believing we've outgrown the teaching of the Bible. So, we appeal to psychology statistics or the latest book some philosopher, theologian, or therapist wrote on the subject. *Hang that!* Give me the Word or give me nothing!

Saints of God, we better settle it once and for all—if we are truly converted, if we love Him with all our hearts—then we better return to the supremacy of Scripture and resolve to let it be the highest authority for our faith and practice, and measure everything in our lives... *everything* we read and hear... **everything,** against *it*, and *never* the other way around.

With every step we take away from Scripture, the more we open ourselves up to teachings like this and slip farther and farther into darkness. I suppose it should not be surprising that we have resorted to burdening the sheep with abominable and unbiblical tripe like urging them to forgive unconditionally, for we have removed repentance from the gospel message.

The doctrine of repentance has become all but extinct in the church. "Repent and believe" has been replaced by "only believe," and even then, "believe" has been altered from its biblical sense. We have honed easy-believism to a new sophistic summit and preach a watered-down gospel that Satan himself would be proud of, in which no one ever needs to repent.

Today repentance is considered offensive. You don't need to renounce your sins and turn from your evil ways. You can simply add Jesus to your collection of idols. We have entire "churches" now comprised of homosexual "believers" who have absolutely no intention of departing from their perverse lifestyle.

You can now walk in open rebellion to God and still call yourself a Christian. "Nevertheless, the firm foundation of God stands, having this seal, 'The Lord knows those who are His,' and, 'Let everyone who names the name of Christ depart from iniquity'" (2 Timothy 2:19).

The church has lost its holy, pilgrim character. We pay lip service to a God we don't know and, rather than crucify the flesh, we dress it up in religious garb . . . and remain inwardly unchanged (forgetting what Jesus taught, that unless our righteousness exceeds that of the scribes and Pharisees, we will *not enter* the kingdom of heaven).

We "appease" God by going to church once or twice a week, but the way we live our lives is really not much different from the world—and don't think they don't know it! They are looking for answers and we don't give them any! Our lives do not reflect the reality of relationship with the living God, through the life-changing, transforming power of the resurrected Lord Jesus Christ, so they look elsewhere—other religions, new age spiritualism, or the latest self-help guru—and they write Christianity off as a farce.

The church is no longer the sanctified company of blood-bought believers who know the redemptive power of Jesus Christ; who know what they have been rescued from; who know their calling, their new identity, and who are committed to walking in that truth; who are growing in grace and godly character; who understand the holy communion of believers and the dynamics of the body—that what one does affects the whole, that if one member suffers, we all suffer; who view sin as a powerful corrosive that destroys our relationship with God and our relationships with one another.

We don't realize the infectious nature of sin and that it will corrupt the whole church, so we see no real urgency in dealing with it. "To each his own," "Don't judge," "We're all just sinners saved by grace," "You gotta forgive 'em" and other mindless mush. These provide ample commentary of the low estate of the church, the bleak and deplorable status quo.

Our thinking is too small. I don't think we understand what's at stake here. This is bigger than you and me. We have lost our vision of the church, the communion of the saints, and Satan has capitalized on it. A flood is spewing out of the dragon's mouth and it's leveled at the whole church, not just a few individual believers. The church of the living God is supposed to be the pillar and support of the truth. We are the living representation of Christ on the earth, His body, His witness to the world, who keep the commandments of God and hold the testimony of Jesus.

There is a reason Scripture is so clear in its teaching on sin and the condition of forgiveness. There is a reason Paul rebuked the Corinthian believers for their complacency in not dealing with the sinner among them, sternly instructing them that, "a little leaven leavens the whole lump" (see 1 Corinthians 5).

There is a reason Jesus laid down very specific ground rules on dealing with a brother who will not repent, and there is a reason he is to be cast outside the company of the holy and loving fellowship of the saints.

There is a reason Jesus taught us to confront and deal with sin rather than ignore it—*for the very same reason we do not ignore cancer!* It is for the sanctity and the preservation of His bride, the protection and vitality of His church! Sin corrodes the fellowship of believers from the inside out. Subversive teachings like unconditional forgiveness weaken the pillars of this sacred community, and bring about its eventual collapse.

The Bible is not unclear about forgiveness. But the devil is cunning. He knows that it's much easier to destroy the church by corrupting it from within, rather than by attacking it from without. From its birth, persecution has only strengthened the church. But by disseminating false doctrines in the church and making them appear biblical (remember, the greatest lie is the one closest to the truth), many have been, and are right now being swept away—especially when those doctrines cultivate complacency and cause us to ignore the cancer of sin, which the doctrine of unconditional forgiveness certainly does!

The church is mighty only when she is holy. We serve a holy God and we are called to be holy ourselves in all our behaviour (1 Peter 1:15, 16; which includes our relationships with one another). What we do affects everyone else in the body (see 1 Corinthians 12).

Remember what happened to the whole nation of Israel because of the sin of one man? They were defeated and chased by their enemies. Because of Achan's sin, the Lord told Joshua, "Therefore the sons of Israel cannot stand before their enemies...for they have become accursed. I will not be with you anymore unless you destroy the things under the ban from your midst" (Joshua 7:12).

God said, "Israel has sinned. I will not go with you, I will not support you, I will not fight for you until you deal with the sin and get rid of it. Remove it from your midst. It has corrupted you. You've been compromised. The hedge is down. Your protection is removed. You can no longer stand before your enemies but will run from them." Can you imagine even for a moment, Joshua instructing the sons of Israel to dole out our insipid, automatic forgiveness to Achan?! Preposterous!

What a sobering lesson this is—for it describes much of the church today! We preen ourselves on our ability to forgive anyone and everyone, thinking this makes us more like Jesus, but we don't realize that we've opened the floodgates to all manner of darkness and filth.

We no longer deal with sin like He taught us to, so truth, sanctity, and the soundness of the church is crumbling all around us. The enemy applauds and all hell rejoices as this doctrine gains momentum. It is sweeping through the church like

49

the plague, and precious few even question it.

Chapter 4

THE NATURE OF SIN

I don't think many of us truly understand the destructive nature of sin. And if you don't understand the nature of sin, you'll never see the need for repentance, or appreciate what a wondrous gift it is. Unconditional forgiveness will never touch the problem of sin and effect reconciliation, for it ignores the source of the problem.

The usual teaching on forgiveness puts pressure on the one *sinned against* to dole out indiscriminate forgiveness, as if that will magically transform the guilty party and restore the broken relationship, but this is a wrong focus. Forgiveness is a *response*, not a catalyst. We have become obsessively preoccupied with the cart (forgiveness), when we should be focusing on the horse (repentance), for without the horse, the cart goes nowhere.

Forgiveness is predicated on repentance, and

if there is no repentance, there is simply nothing to forgive. Imagine going to your favorite restaurant where you are seated and eagerly look forward to a fine meal. The waiter comes and sets an empty plate before you and says, "Enjoy your meal." You would rightly respond, "What meal? What are you talking about? You didn't bring me anything!"

So it is with forgiveness. Until there is repentance, there is *nothing* to forgive. That's why Jesus taught us to go to such lengths in bringing about a sinning brother's repentance—all of which is utterly pointless and is completely circumvented by unconditional forgiveness.

The goal of repentance and forgiveness is the restoration of a damaged relationship. It was damaged by sin. That was the cause. So it can only begin to be repaired by repentance—a change of heart in the person that caused the damage. When there is repentance, only then is the proper response (to the person) forgiveness, and the result is a restoration of the relationship to holy love, truth, and righteousness.

When we psychologize the teaching of the Bible we dilute its vital truth and power. It is no wonder the so-called spiritual principles we try to implement in our lives simply don't work. We have deluded ourselves by making repentance merely a way to assuage our guilt, a means to soothe our stinging conscience. But this is not the objective of repentance. This is false repentance for the object is still self.

When we sin against God, the purpose of repentance is not a selfish one, though the results greatly benefit us. The object is *God*. The goal of repentance is that it restores us to a right relationship with Him.

Similarly, we have psychologized forgiveness. We have reduced it to nothing more than a cheap self-help device, a crude coping mechanism in the face of someone else's sin. I have heard teachers counsel forgiveness merely as a path to inward peace, a way to make *ourselves* feel better, or to avoid the peril of bitterness (which we will discuss below). This is horribly ineffective at best, for we have abandoned the teaching of Scripture and the divine purpose of forgiveness.

It is important to understand the dynamic of sin. "Your iniquities have made a separation between you and your God, and your sins have hidden His face from you, so that He does not hear" (Isaiah 59:2). Sin separates us from God and it separates us from one another. It breaks the chain, the connection, the bond between people, and drives a wedge between them. It causes a breach in the relationship, and that breach does not just go away on its own. "A brother offended is harder to be won than a strong city" (Prov. 18:19).[6]

Sin damages the bridge, the relationship between ourselves and others. And no amount of forced forgiveness on our part can repair the bridge. Only repentance can do that. The offense is still out there *until* the offender repents. There's nothing *we* can do about *their* offense (aside from confronting them and following our Lord's instructions in Luke

---

6   Incidentally, we see in this verse that the onus is on the offender to win back the person he has offended.

17 and Matthew 18). That's *why* we confront them. It's an effort to repair the bridge. But make no mistake, if they refuse to repent, the relationship remains severed, and all the forgiveness in the world will not restore it.

God does not expect us, as a fallback position, to resort to reframing and denial or other psycho-stupid banalities and pseudo-spiritual absurdities to pretend the offense never happened or to force ourselves merely to *forgive and forget*. This does nothing to facilitate restoration. It only trivializes the nature of sin, tears down the standard of truth and righteousness, and contributes to the crippling of the body, the disintegration of the church. Urging a believer to forgive an unrepentant offender puts a burden on them that neither God, the church, nor their own conscience can bear.

Chapter 5

THE NECESSITY OF

REPENTANCE

The votaries of unconditional forgiveness regard repentance as unnecessary and even irrelevant in the forgiveness process. They insist the Bible teaches that forgiveness should be dispensed regardless of the offender's state of heart—even in the face of stubborn unrepentance. We have clearly seen that this is ludicrous.

Teaching a forgiveness which ignores the offender's attitude is not only foolish and disobedient (for we openly disregard the teaching of Scripture), but we do the saints of God (especially those sinned against) a great disservice by obscuring and even eliminating the standard of truth and righteousness. Ultimately, this puts a stumbling block before both the one sinned against *and* the offender.

Repentance makes no sense if there is no standard of truth and righteousness, for what are we to return to? Whose standard do we live by? Repentance has fallen into disuse because we have lowered the holy standard of God's word. Have you never wondered why our apathetic, anemic brand of Christianity, and much of the church, bears little or no resemblance to biblical teaching?

By lowering the standard of truth, the biblical teaching on repentance *and* forgiveness must be changed. The problem of sin will not go away on its own. Jesus assured His disciples, "It is inevitable that stumbling blocks should come." He never said we would be without offenses. That's why He prepared us by telling us *how* to deal with them. He did not leave us in the dark. And He certainly did not leave it up to our fickle emotions and sentimentalized notions of love.

If we reject our Lord's teaching and adopt the vapid, enervating teachings of men, instead of dealing with offenses God's way, then we must invent passive and pathetic ways of coping with the problem. Exit repentance stage right. Enter unconditional forgiveness stage left. This is what happens when we depart from the teaching of Scripture.

A theology professor once told me that repentance was a Pauline concept and that Jesus never preached repentance. After recovering from the shock of such an assertion, I opened my Bible to Mark 1:15 and read to him that repentance was *the Lord's message* from the start. Other references began flooding my mind (e.g. Matt. 4:17; 11:20-24; 12:38-41; 21:28-32; Mk. 6:12; Lk. 5:32; 13:1-5; 15; 17:3, 4; 24:47; Rev. 2:5, 16, 22; 3:3, 19), and I found myself wondering how he could believe something so far off base.[7]

Repentance is a foundational Christian doctrine. When the church strays from its foundations, it suffers dearly. You can't become (or remain) a Christian without repentance. Without having a foundation of repentance, we cannot press on to maturity in the faith (Hebrews 6:1). In fact, the Christian life could be called, in one sense, a walk of repentance, in that it is a progressive turning from sin and turning to God.

Though some view repentance in a negative light, I consider it a great gift from God and cherish it deeply. When I fall, it is indeed a wondrous and loving provision to be able to run to my Father to be cleansed and restored to a right relationship with Him. When I sin against my brother or sister, it is amazing to see what happens when I honor them enough to go to them in humility, acknowledge my sin, admitting and fully confessing my wrong, and ask for their forgiveness. Only in this way can restoration truly begin.

I hope that by better understanding the nature of sin, as we looked at in the last chapter, you

---

7 He had made other assertions such as, "There were no women baptized in the Bible" (apparently being unfamiliar with Acts 8:12; 16:13-15), in a feeble attempt to justify infant baptism. This is troubling, and makes me question whether the word of God truly has precedence in our faith and practice over personal and denominational biases. For I do not believe these statements come from a mind soaked in Scripture.

can begin to see the importance and necessity of repentance. When the bridge is damaged, all the forgiveness in the world can't repair it. Repentance is the only thing that can begin to repair the bridge to someone we have sinned against.

Through the ages, repentance was the resounding message of the prophets. It was the clarion message of the Lord's forerunner, John the Baptist. It was the consistent message of our Lord Himself and His apostles. And it was (and is) the message of every man and woman of God who ever lived, because without this precious gift and benevolent provision from our heavenly Father, there *is* no good news. There is no way out. We are still in our sins. "The soul who sins will die...Turn back, turn back from your evil ways! Why then will you die, O house of Israel?...Therefore, repent and live" (Ezekiel 18:4, 32; 33:11). Repentance is our way out.

The blood of Jesus paid the full price and penalty for our sins but without repentance, we will never access the merits of His redemptive work, nor reap the slightest benefit. Repentance opens the door to the kingdom and heart of God. When we besmear repentance with sludge like unconditional forgiveness, we essentially close the door and cut off access to God from those who need Him most—those entangled in sin. In this way, *we* become the stumbling blocks Jesus warned His disciples about. We do this in two ways.

First, we put a stumbling block before the one *sinned against* by trivializing the offense. By negating the offender's accountability and pressuring the offended to "forgive anyway," we overburden the conscience of the offended party and ignore the clear biblical directives in how to deal with sin. We show that we are not fully committed to obeying the truth of God's word and we leave the contagion of sin unchecked. Aside from the pestilential effects on the whole community, we expose the one sinned against more acutely to the fiery darts of the evil one, making them more vulnerable to the temptation of bitterness and resentment.[8] This is no small matter.

Second, we also put a stumbling block before *the offender*. We trivialize his offense and negate his accountability to a higher standard, and thus do violence to the standard itself (the word of God). When we do not hold him accountable, we send the message that there *is* no standard of truth and righteousness (or that it is not necessary to obey it!).

We also send the message that there is no consequence for his sin. It's like saying, "It's okay to drink poison." While the effects of sin may not be as immediate or visible, they're most definitely there. His sin has separated him from God, has released a virulent, corrupting influence in his life, and has moved him out from under the canopy of grace to be tormented by the powers of darkness. This can only be stopped by repentance but our puerile attitudes about forgiveness no longer require this, so we leave him in darkness.[9]

We not only tear down the standard of truth and leave him in his sin, separated from God, the

---

8 We shall discuss this temptation more fully in chapter 7.
9 Despite those who insist that indiscriminate forgiveness is the loving and merciful thing to do, in truth it is neither.

very source of life and peace, but we also misrepresent God. When we forgive without repentance, we communicate that God does too. The offender need not repent therefore, because God has already forgiven him! Thus, *we* put a great stumbling block before him by obscuring the truth and distorting the character of God.

The offender's own conscience and innate, God-given sense of justice tells him there is something wrong with this. But we persist in our delusions to forgive and pass along our deceit. The net result: We suppress the truth before him, we check the conviction of the Holy Spirit within him urging him to repent, and we actually lead him astray.

God wants us to repent. This should be our natural reaction when we fall. The Lord asks, "Do men fall and not get up again? Does one turn away and not repent?" (Jeremiah 8:4). The Spirit of God is working in the offender to bring him to repentance but we, like the false prophets of old, turn him aside, saying in effect, "Peace, peace," when there is no peace. We remove the hope of restoration and block his way back to God. We hide the key of repentance and bar the door. We actually shut off the kingdom from him.

Jesus gave us clear instructions in order to bring about his repentance, and we disregard and nullify all of them by treating repentance as if it were *unnecessary*.

There is a reason in the higher wisdom of God that Jesus taught us to confront and deal with sin! How dare we treat His word as if it were merely optional, and think we can casually ignore His teachings. We must repent of our wicked arrogance in thinking we are wiser than the God of all truth and knowledge! The church is suffering immensely because of our disobedience.

The fundamental, unchanging prerequisite of forgiveness has always been, and always will be, **repentance**. It can be no other way. *This* is the incontrovertible teaching of Scripture. We are never told to forgive unconditionally. This resolves nothing. God does not forgive us unless we repent, and nowhere does He instruct us to forgive others without the very same condition. He is always our model and we follow His example.

Chapter 6

"BUT WHAT ABOUT THAT
PRAYER OF JESUS?"

Whenever I discuss this teaching, someone will invariably ask, "But what about when Jesus prayed, 'Father, forgive them; for they do not know what they are doing?'" It's a fair question worthy of an honest answer.

For many, this verse is the linchpin in the doctrine of unconditional forgiveness. It seems to be the primary girder supporting this doctrine. When confronted with the truths in this book, they are quick to cite this verse thinking to trump and silence any and all argument.

This prayer appears only in Luke's Gospel (23:34). Imagine my surprise when I discovered it was not original to his Gospel but were added later. *was* That means these words *did not come from Luke's quill!* If you have a good study Bible, there should be a note stating that these words were a later addition to the text, that the earliest manuscripts do not contain this verse, or something to that effect.[10]

Of course, most people do not realize this. And many who do, sort of gloss over the fact because this intercalated prayer fits in nicely with their mawkish conception of who Jesus is and what they *think* He would say. This is yet another example of how we have sentimentalized the Lord Jesus and the word of God.

Learning that this verse was added some time after Luke wrote his Gospel made sense because it simply doesn't fit. The text flows more naturally without these words. No loss of meaning occurs by skipping them. A sensitive reading gives one the sense that these words were inserted later by someone other than Luke.

Moreover, these words do not harmonize with the broader testimony of Scripture. Most people believe this dubious prayer was uttered for the benefit of the Pharisees, those ultimately responsible for our Lord's death, to absolve the unthinkable crescendo of their wickedness.

But this simply does not jell with the Lord's words elsewhere. It is inconceivable that Jesus would here pray for them to be forgiven on the basis

---

10 This verse has double brackets in my Greek New Testament, with a note explaining that this passage was a later addition to the text. In his *Textual Commentary on the Greek New Testament,* Metzger provides an array of early and diverse witnesses, affirming that the absence of these words from those manuscripts "is most impressive and can scarcely be explained as a deliberate excision by copyists." He concedes they were not part of the original Gospel of Luke and were added later by unknown copyists.

of their ignorance, when everything else He had told them was that they *would* be held accountable for their deeds and punished most severely.[11]

The Pharisees had never shown themselves to be anything *but* completely given over to evil, hate, murder, and corruption—so much so, that Jesus told them bluntly, "You are like whitewashed tombs...full of dead men's bones and all uncleanness...you are full of hypocrisy and lawlessness" (Matthew 23:27, 28). Their corruption prompted the Lord to ask them a searing rhetorical question, "You serpents, you brood of vipers, *how shall you escape the sentence of hell?*" (Matthew 23:33).

They were oppressing men with heavy burdens and shutting off the kingdom of heaven from them. They were blind guides who did not know God and opposed, persecuted and killed those who did. They never showed even the slightest hint of humility, brokenness, and repentance? Jesus made it unequivocally clear that they were wicked (*sons of Satan!* John 8:44; cf. Matthew 23:15), that they were filling up the measure of their guilt and racing toward judgment (Matthew 23:32-36; cf. 1 Thessalonians 2:14-16).

Then, in one sentence, Jesus contradicts all that He had repeatedly told them—*because they didn't know any better?!* Not a chance! This spurious prayer is a bizarre note, strikingly off-key, shrill and discordant in the symphony of His life and ministry. God has never forgiven those who are stubborn, hardhearted, and unrepentant. His

---

11 See, for example, Matt. 23:1-36; Lk. 11:43-51; Jn. 19:11; Lk. 20: 45-47 (NIV); Matt. 21:28-45!

consistent plea has been for them to repent, so that He can!

Moreover, it is unlikely that Jesus would make a strange and sudden provision for ignorance when He had never done so before. For even the ignorance and blindness of the Pharisees, Jesus told them, was due to their sin, their pride and hardness of heart. Thus, they were culpable and would most assuredly be held accountable. The only cure for their ignorance was repentance.

In another place, Jesus did say that punishment would be more lenient for those who did not know their master's will and committed deeds worthy of stripes, but it must be noted that they were still punished—*not forgiven*. He did *not* say that because they did not know any better, their sins would not be held against them, that they would be absolved of their guilt (Luke 12:47, 48).

After our Lord's resurrection, the transformed, Spirit-filled Peter removed all doubt about the guilt of the Pharisees—their ignorance notwithstanding. He did not mince words or concern himself with subtlety. Feel the force of his indictments! "Whom *you* crucified!" "Whom *you* had put to death by hanging Him on a cross" (Acts 4:10; 5:30).

He implicated all the Jewish people as well, saying, "whom *you* nailed to a cross" (Acts 2:23, 36). Then, after healing the lame man at the Beautiful Gate of the temple, when all the people "were filled with wonder and amazement," Peter again seized the opportunity to accuse them, "...But *you* disowned the Holy and Righteous One, and asked for a murderer to be granted to you, but put to death the Prince of life...." (Acts 3:14, 15).

Now get this! "And now, brethren, I know that you *acted in ignorance*, just as your rulers did also" (Acts 3:17). But did he excuse their ignorance? Did he tell them they were already forgiven, or would be forgiven because they didn't know any better? No! He conceded their ignorance, *yet still called them to repent*, knowing that this was the only door to forgiveness.

Listen to the Holy Spirit's response to their ignorance through the mouth of Peter, "**Repent therefore and return, that** your sins *may* be wiped away, in order that times of refreshing *may* come from the presence of the Lord..." (Acts 3:14-19). Notice the word *may* here. *May* implies a condition. It's not a guarantee. Only a fool would assume the latter promises of this verse could occur without the former condition being met. So, once again, we see that the condition of their forgiveness was plainly repentance.

From everything we read about the Pharisees, the repeated woes and judgments pronounced upon them by John the Baptist, the Lord Jesus Himself, and the apostles after the Lord's resurrection, we see that they were hardened enemies of all truth and righteousness, who stubbornly opposed the gospel and were indeed "filling up the measure of their guilt," in crucifying our Lord.

They had callously cried out, "His blood be on us and on our children!" (Matthew 27:25). And that is precisely what happened to those who did not repent, for "the Lord will by no means leave the guilty unpunished" (Nahum 1:3; Proverbs 11:21 NIV).

Finally, the Lord's prophecies about the destruction of Jerusalem are decidedly inconsistent with this supposed prayer. With chilling solemnity, Jesus said, "O Jerusalem, Jerusalem, who kills the prophets and stones those who are sent to her! How often I wanted to gather your children together, the way a hen gathers her chicks under her wings, and *you were unwilling.* Behold, your house is being *left to you desolate!*" (Matthew 23:38). There is an eerie finality to His words.

Jesus had come to Jerusalem for the last time. He came to His own and His own did not receive Him. When Jesus left the Temple, He never returned! The temple was left a mere building without God's presence, no different than the temple of Zeus or Artemis.

Jesus said "When you see Jerusalem surrounded by armies, then know that her desolation (destruction) is near . . . this is the time of punishment . . . There will be great distress upon the land and wrath against this people" (Luke 21:20-24).

Listen to the Lord's terrifying prediction of doom. "As He approached Jerusalem and saw the city, He wept over it, saying, 'If you had only known on this day what would bring you peace! But now it is hidden from your eyes. For the days shall come upon you when your enemies will throw up a bank before you, and surround you, and hem you in on every side, and will level you to the ground and the children within you, and they will not leave in you one stone upon another" Why? **because you did not recognize the time of your visitation**" (Luke

19:41-44).

This occurred not forty years hence in 70 A.D. Jerusalem was sacked by the Romans and the temple was burnt. In meticulous fulfillment of the Lord's prophecy, not one stone was left upon another. Early Christians saw this as God's judgment on the Jews for rejecting and crucifying the Lord Jesus. The first-century Jewish historian, Josephus, provides a first-hand account. He relates the fulfillment of the Lord's prophecy in awful detail in his first work, *The Wars of the Jews* (or *The History of the Destruction of Jerusalem*), published about 75 A.D.

Let's suppose for a moment, just for the sake of argument, that Jesus did pray these words. First of all, it seems perfectly clear from the context, that He's referring to the soldiers who were for the most part simply carrying out orders and doing their job. That would at least make more sense of this prayer.

But if these words were indeed penned by Luke, would it change anything? No indeed! I am amazed at how much people accept and how much they're willing to reject on the basis of this one verse. They embrace an entire doctrinal edifice teetering primarily on this verse to the astonishing neglect of the Lord's plain teaching elsewhere. Jesus told His disciples to make disciples of all nations, *teaching them to obey **all** that I commanded you* (Matthew 28:19, 20).

The well-attested teaching sections of Jesus should preeminently govern the conduct of believers and the ethics of the church. Are we actually willing to disregard the clear teaching of our Lord (e.g. in Matthew 18 and Luke 17:3, 4) on the basis of this verse?

Regarding these words Jesus supposedly prayed, it is indeed baffling that they could be added later by some anonymous scribe and still be considered part of the Gospel of *Luke!* I can't explain to you how verses like this found their way into the text of your Bible. I'll leave that to the scholars.

What I *can* tell you is that to the unbiased, this verse conflicts with the greater testimony of Scripture. And, that it's profoundly unwise to ignore our Lord's clear teaching about forgiveness on the basis of one dubious verse.

Chapter 7

"BUT WHAT ABOUT

BITTERNESS?"

Exposing A False Dichotomy

A fail-safe is something that is designed to engage at the point of failure in order to prevent the breakdown of a mechanism. It is a secondary system, a contingency plan, if you will, that insures continued operation even if the primary system fails.

So also with false doctrines. It has been a sobering observation to recognize the fail-safes consistently present in false teachings. It reveals that far from being accidental, there is indeed a mastermind behind all error. The enemy builds fail-safes into false teachings to make them look more plausible and to evade detection.

This serves to insulate people further from the

truth and make it harder for them to escape the bondage of his deception. He does not give up captives easily. He capitalizes on our ignorance and feeds on our fear. And sadly, the more tenderhearted and sincere a believer is (until he develops strong discernment and a solid biblical foundation), the more vulnerable he or she is to the cunning wiles of the deceiver.

As with all false doctrines, the enemy has built fail-safes into *this* doctrine as well. One of the most effective of these is the fear of bitterness. A strong fear it is too, for it has kept many in bondage. If one should dare to question the absurdity of unconditional forgiveness, this fail-safe engages, stamps out all doubt and questioning, checks their retreat, and beats them back into submission. Many believe that bitterness is the antithesis of forgiveness, the unavoidable pitfall and inevitable consequence of unforgiveness. They believe this because this is what they have been taught by deceived Christian leaders.

This fear has become so deeply ingrained in them that they wince in horror at the very thought of not forgiving someone, as if they were standing at the edge of a precipice on a blustery day, certain that at any moment they will be blown over and dashed on the jagged rocks of bitterness below. But this simply is not true. This erroneous belief only keeps you ensnared in this doctrine. The enemy has succeeded in building a fail-safe here, through those who parrot this doctrine, by setting up a false dichotomy, which serves to strengthen compliance.

I shudder to think how many teachings I have

heard on forgiveness where the "forgiveness/bitterness" dichotomy is presented in a scary, "If you don't forgive, you're bitter!" dynamic. It really is quite predictable. This severely reductionist treatment has indeed vexed and flayed many a tender conscience.

I have talked with many who have bought into this lie, and have fervently (and fearfully) embraced this dichotomy. Afraid of being bitter, and convinced that bitterness is the only outcome of unforgiveness, sincere believers run wildly to the other extreme and force themselves, through some bizarre emotional contortionism, to forgive someone who has sinned against them, even though the biblical condition of forgiveness has not been met. We must be careful of thinking in extremes. Truth is rarely found there.

When confronted with the truths in this book, someone will invariably ask the question posed in the title of this chapter, "But what about bitterness?" This usually springs more from a deep-seated fear of being rejected by God than from a heart to quibble with the truth of what I'm saying.

So, let me be clear. Am I in any way encouraging or advocating a spirit of malice, rancor, venom, or revenge? Perish the thought! A bitter, rancorous, vindictive spirit is never of God. But this only further illustrates my point. If the Bible teaches that we are *not* to forgive unconditionally, then it certainly cannot follow that bitterness is our only recourse. This cannot be shown from any biblical text.

What gives power to this fail-safe is that it has been cast in an over-simplified antithesis, a crude *either/or*. But these are *not* our only two options. When you do not forgive (because the offender refuses to repent), I am not suggesting that you nurse a grudge instead, and it does *not* mean that you will automatically be thrown upon the rocks of bitterness. The reason I call this a false dichotomy is quite simply because it is *not true.*

The Bible does not support this dichotomy, therefore it too must be rejected as part of this godless doctrine. Your conscience need not be in bondage to fear, simply by following our Lord's teachings. This is yet another devious trick of the enemy to get you to abandon the truth of Scripture.

The text most commonly appealed to (warning against a root of bitterness) is taken from Hebrews 12:14-17. This passage has been used as a sort of theological club, a spiritual scare tactic to warn of the dangers (and the supposedly *inevitable* consequence) of unforgiveness.

What is frightening is how often I have heard this passage used in this way (*even by seminary professors who really ought to know better!*). It may surprise you to learn—indeed it is profoundly appalling to learn—that this passage has *absolutely* **nothing to do with unforgiveness!** Did you get that? *Nothing!* It has been shamelessly hijacked and egregiously mutilated in a way that once again (as we've seen so many times above) does violence to the true meaning of the passage.

Like wolves tearing bits of flesh from a carcass until it is no longer known what they are tearing it from, pieces are torn from this passage to fashion a new meaning, one which bears no resemblance to the original. This passage has been made to say something like, "If you don't forgive, a root of bitterness will grow in you and it will defile you." That certainly sounds scary.

And those who wish to give the warning a finer point will make some comparison to Esau being rejected (because of the root that grew in him). A sincere conscience completely caves at the thought of being rejected!! So out of fear, we do everything we can to forgive anyone and everyone with a blanket, wholesale, indiscriminate forgiveness, which looks *nothing like biblical forgiveness*. Saints of God, I am deeply grieved that you have been troubled in this way. Hear the truth of this passage, step out of the darkness and feel the balm of the Holy Spirit comfort your souls:

> Pursue peace with all men, and holiness without which **no one** will see the Lord. See to it that **no one** comes short of the grace of God; that **no root** of bitterness springing up causes trouble, and by it many become defiled; that there be **no** immoral or godless **person** like Esau, who sold his birthright for a single meal. For you know that even afterwards, when he desired to inherit the blessing, he was rejected, for he found no place for repentance, though he sought for it with tears.

It is readily apparent after even a cursory reading of this passage that there is not the vaguest reference to unforgiveness, so I need not expound at length. Just a few observations will suffice. You will notice I have emphasized certain words in the passage with bold font. This is to highlight the first important observation, which is that a root of bitterness is not something that grows *in* a person. It *is* a person!

This root of bitterness is a person in the assembly of believers who defiles others. This language is taken from Moses who warned God's people of old, the Israelites, against idolatry and apostasy. "Beware lest there be among you **a man or woman or family or tribe**, whose heart turns away this day from the Lord our God to go and serve the gods of those nations; lest there be among [*not in*] you **a root** bearing poisonous and bitter fruit" (Deuteronomy 29:18 RSV). The book of Hebrews is addressing the danger of apostasy, and the writer repeatedly warns (Jewish) believers against abandoning their faith in Jesus.

Far from encouraging a passive, blind, generic forgiveness for all, and warning against the consequences of unforgiveness, this passage teaches us to walk in holiness, active discipleship, and discernment in watching out for one another. It warns of allowing someone like this—an immoral or godless person like Esau, a poisonous and bitter root, a defector—to dwell in their midst. For that root will defile others in the church.

This is a parallel passage to 1 Corinthians 5, which is about safeguarding the sanctity and integrity of the believing community by dealing with those *through whom* the rest of the body becomes corrupted (defiled). This is precisely why our Lord gave us explicit instructions (which are not optional!) on how to deal with sin in others—instructions which are totally subverted if we forgive unconditionally.

The wisdom of our Lord's teaching is that when we are sinned against, He gave us very clear steps to follow to facilitate restoration, which can only happen if the offender repents. This obviously allows for the possibility that he may *not* repent, which means we *do not forgive*—out of simple obedience to our Lord's teaching! This cannot mean then that our only alternative is to fall headlong into bitterness.

Remember above, when David said, "God is good, ready to forgive...?" In the same way, we are to maintain a willingness, *a readiness* to forgive, just as God does, and this can be done without holding a grudge and without bitterness and resentment poisoning our hearts.

We must keep our hearts pure and broken before God, but if we forgive prematurely, we circumvent the convicting work of the Holy Spirit in the offender's heart, thwart the will of God in the situation, leaving the rest of the body exposed to the corruption of sin, and we fail to deal with the real problem.

We must pray earnestly throughout. We must commit our hearts to God, and resolve to honor His word and walk in His truth—even against our own fear-motivated impulse to forgive. He will guard our hearts and keep us in His name. He has not left us alone. "He keeps the feet of His saints," (1 Samuel 2:9) and "He will not allow your foot to slip" (Psalm 121:3). His grace *is* sufficient for us and we *can* by the Spirit walk in obedience through the steps Jesus outlined.

If there is no repentance after confronting a brother or sister about their sin, the next step is to take one or two more. Perhaps one of the reasons we engage others in the process is for strength and support, and to help keep *us* accountable, so that we maintain God's perspective over our own. Also, to keep the process from devolving into mere quarrels and personal vendettas.

Our principal objective is always, first and foremost, the will of God. Of course, this assumes that those whom we enlist in this process are mature, fully committed to God and the truth of His word.

Do not enlist the help of those who are fickle and prone to partiality, but those led by the Spirit who are supremely committed to walking in truth (which most assuredly disqualifies those who are drunk on the wine of this false doctrine). Otherwise, things can go desperately awry.

I have heard tragic accounts where a person attempted to deal with an unrepentant offender according to our Lord's instructions. Being spurned by the offender, they enlisted others, and then ultimately the elders in their church, only to be sloughed off in a most appalling manner and pressured to forgive. They were made to think *they* were the source of the problem and that *they* were sinning against God *by not forgiving!*

This is an egregious abuse of spiritual authority and an enormous stumbling block to the one sinned against. They were simply trying to obey our Lord's teaching, and disobedient leaders rebuffed and chastened them for it.

As a result, those sinned against become engulfed in a cloud of confusion and despair, exposed to severe attacks by the enemy, and made vastly more vulnerable to the temptation of bitterness—all because of a blatant disregard of God's Word.

If we pay lip service to the truth we profess to love but disengage at the critical moment of obedience to that truth, how are we different in any appreciable way from the Pharisees who indulged their own private notions of religion, disconnected from the reality of God and His word? Jesus said if our righteousness does not exceed theirs we will not enter the kingdom of heaven (Matthew 5:20).

He also said, "Woe to him through whom [stumbling blocks] come! It would be better for him if a millstone were hung around his neck and he were thrown into the sea, than that he should cause one of these little ones to stumble" (Luke 17:1, 2). *Take heed!*

The abuses of our Lord's instruction to confront sin have indeed been several and varied. Sometimes our Lord's teaching has been misused by corrupt shepherds and a power-mad ecclesiastical hierarchy to control and dominate the sheep, to whip them into submission to an egotistical leader or cult-like group. This is known as spiritual abuse, and I have seen firsthand the effects of this.

But the several abuses should never cause us to neglect and abandon the truth. Many leaders have perhaps become complacent in obeying the truth *because of* abuses, and deem it much easier to urge a wholesale forgiveness, and to hold the charge (fear) of bitterness over the heads of believers like a club, than to follow the clear teaching of Scripture. But they shall account to God for this wrong.

An unbiblical "forgive no matter what" campaign does not come without a price. We cannot depart from scriptural truth without paying dearly for it. We have short-circuited the process. It can be messy to follow the Lord's instructions, so many have opted to do it their way...and are reaping the pathetic results.

We don't go through the trouble of actually dealing with sin anymore, as Jesus taught us to do, but then the church in our day doesn't look very much like the New Testament church either. Riddled with compromise, tolerance, and false love, so as to accommodate the world, and the steady erosion of all that is holy and pure has made it harder and harder to discern the true church at all. But I digress.

Aside from the passage in Hebrews discussed above, bitterness is only mentioned three times in the New Testament, and interestingly, *never in connection with, and certainly not as the inevitable consequence of* not forgiving someone.

Paul does not appear to be concerned about bitterness when he rebuked the believers in Corinth for not dealing with the sinner among them (1 Corinthians 5). He commanded them to remove the offender from their midst and to refuse any association with him until he repented—without any mention of bitterness. He commanded them not even to eat with someone who claims to be a brother but is immoral or covetous and so on! How many churches today do you know that take this biblical command seriously?!

The Lord Jesus did not warn His disciples of bitterness when He gave them instructions about dealing with an erring brother (or sister) in Matthew 18 or Luke 17, where one would most expect to see this caution. If this dichotomy were true, He would surely have said something here. He allowed for the obvious possibility that we would *not forgive* in the event of unrepentance, but not one word was uttered about bitterness being the inevitable consequence. So much for the dichotomy.

Our Lord is not remiss. He never said, "In following My instructions here, I must tell you, the brother who sinned against you may not repent. Thus you are not to forgive, but make sure you guard against bitterness, because when you do not forgive, you will be exposed to this temptation most acutely."

We do not read anything like that. Not so much as a passing mention. So, obviously, there is considerable space between not forgiving an unrepentant brother and the danger of being swallowed up in bitterness.

Bitterness is a choice. We do not *have to be* bitter. We can resist this just like any other godless attitude. It is not a simple *either/or*. So throw off the yoke of this error and embrace the truth.

One of the primary reasons bitterness has become a major concern, and this false dichotomy constructed, is precisely *because* we have removed repentance from the process. We discussed this extensively above. When we take something away, we have to put something in its place.

81

If you're being pressured to forgive an unrepentant offender, and no one agrees to confront him and hold him accountable for his actions, this is a glaring failure in the body of Christ. It's a clear violation of the teaching of Scripture and a perversion of truth and justice. If the Spirit of God dwells in you, how can you *not* feel outraged? Where do you think that sense of justice and righteousness comes from?

Remaining passive and trying to muster up forgiveness while the Spirit of God within you is grieved, and is urging obedience to His word, results inevitably in your feeling conflicted.

Those who embrace this false "forgiveness/bitterness" dichotomy do not understand the sense of justice and righteous indignation that wells up in the heart of every true child of God in the face of sin. They wrongly equate it with bitterness. But that is ridiculous. God (and His Spirit dwelling within us) hates sin. I am forced to wonder about those who have any other reaction, whose spirit they're of.

The beauty of our Lord's teaching is that it fully recognizes the destructive nature of sin. He does not attempt to trivialize it and sweep it under the rug. He does not direct us to walk in denial, to minimize or psychologize the offense (or our response to it), to rationalize and justify the offender, to resort to reframing and emotional casuistry, to forgive merely to soothe our own emotions or to avoid the peril of bitterness, or any other such folly.

We are not without recourse, which in itself

provides an effective safeguard against bitterness. Our Lord's instructions fully acknowledge the evil and wrongfulness of sin, and are aimed squarely at bringing about the repentance of the offender and the reconciliation of relationships. And in this we are consoled.

We must come to recognize that there are times and situations where it is simply *wrong* to forgive, and bitterness is *not* the inevitable result. Jesus told His disciples, "If you forgive the sins of any, their sins have been forgiven them; *if you retain the sins of any, they have been retained*" (John 20:23).

Why retain the sins of some? Why not just forgive 'em all, like the proponents of unconditional forgiveness insist we should do? Because obviously not everyone will repent, so their sin remains until they do.

However you interpret this verse, it is clear that we are not to forgive everyone automatically. In this "retaining the sins of some," which is essentially *unforgiveness* (though interestingly, this term never appears in Scripture), you might note that Jesus did not utter one word about bitterness. Again, so much for the dichotomy!

The same act can be either good or evil, depending on the situation and motive of the one performing it.[12] So it is with forgiveness or

---

12 For example, the prayers and alms-giving of the Pharisees, because of their evil motives, were evil, and so rejected by God. But these same acts, when done from a pure heart, are good and acceptable in the sight of God. In fact, we are commanded to do them.

unforgiveness. There are times when forgiveness is the right and proper course of action, and there are times when it very clearly is not. There are times when unforgiveness is evil, and there are times when it is the indisputable will of God, and bitterness need never enter into it.

This false dichotomy has no basis in Scripture. It was a fail-safe designed to keep people enslaved to this godless doctrine. And so, like anything that causes us to stray from the truth of God's word, we must roundly reject it.

Chapter 8

THE OMINOUS IMPLICATIONS

OF THIS DOCTRINE

The doctrine of unconditional forgiveness is not only unbiblical and gravely detrimental to the church, but the implications of this doctrine effectively strip off its mawkish mask to reveal the true face of its apostate nature.

    The professor who penned the insipid article on forgiveness above (ch. 3), said in his article, "Like the gospel itself forgiveness must be free." This is precisely the sort of doublespeak that has kept many sincere believers befuddled and ensnared in this doctrine. They are seduced by this quasi noble, high-sounding gibberish, without actually thinking it through to its logical conclusion. Let me try to untangle this theological pretzel-thinking, and lead you out of this dark labyrinth.

The gospel is *not* free, at least not in the sense the professor asserts, using *free* interchangeably with *unconditional,* like the forgiveness he advocates. Someone had to pay the price for our sin. It cost God His beloved Son, and He has laid down a very specific entrance requirement—*condition* if you will—for admittance into His kingdom, which we shall return to in a moment.

The gospel *is* free in the sense that we cannot earn it based on our own merits (otherwise, Christ died in vain). But it is *not* unconditional, meaning that we get it *no matter what.* This is false synonymy. The professor confuses terms, and in so doing, reveals a severe geological fault in the foundation of this doctrine, showing conclusively that at its core, it is fundamentally unsound and *unbiblical.*

The terms "free" and "unconditional" are *not* interchangeable, but the professor's careless melding actually helps us here, for he unwittingly and fortuitously uncovers a grave error hidden in the DNA of unconditional forgiveness, with serious implications. Setting forth a forgiveness that is unconditional, that eliminates the need for repentance, and then comparing it to the gospel itself, is chilling.

Making repentance unnecessary while at the same time insisting that we forgive the person anyway, freely and unconditionally—if this be our model, then it means everyone *is* (or will be) forgiven, even *without repentance!* And since this "free" forgiveness is modeled on the "free" gospel itself, repentance then becomes insignificant and totally irrelevant. It really doesn't matter if anyone repents because they're forgiven unconditionally.

Carried to its logical conclusion, if everyone is forgiven and not accountable for their sins, meaning their sins are of no consequence, then everyone is (or will be) saved. And this, my friends, is an age-old heresy called Universalism. *This* is the outcome and final destination of this doctrine, the true apostate face of unconditional forgiveness. And its widespread acceptance represents a singular triumph for the kingdom of darkness.

Let it be said clearly, soberly, and emphatically, that Universalism is *not* the gospel of Jesus Christ! Its precursor, unconditional forgiveness, also is NOT the teaching of Jesus Christ.

Neither the gospel nor forgiveness is unconditional. Never was. Never will be. The consistent and repeated calls to repentance throughout Scripture would make absolutely no sense if forgiveness were unconditional. Repentance is the invariable, fundamental condition for admittance into the kingdom of God. Scripture is abundantly clear on this. Jesus said it perhaps most succinctly when He confirmed that, "Unless you repent, you will all likewise perish" (Luke 13:1-5).

The eternal, unchanging truth is that no one will get into the kingdom of God without repenting and "bringing forth the fruit of repentance." This is the essential, unalterable condition set forth by our Lord. No one is forgiven who does not repent. The gospel is therefore not in this sense "free."

In fact, the gospel is not even good news . . . to *everyone*. For while it is incomparably good news to sinners who repent and believe (like the full pardon of one sentenced to death), it holds out the worst news, yea the certainty of eternal punishment and endless torment (unquenchable fire and never-ending agony where "there shall be weeping and gnashing of teeth") to sinners who refuse to repent. Make no mistake, there will *be* no devils and no sinners in heaven. You can be sure of that. The doors of the kingdom remain forever barred to the unrepentant.

CONCLUSION

I confess, when I began writing this book, the panoply of notes and journal entries strewn about my desk, I believed strongly in the truths here presented, but not so much as I do now. In the process of writing, praying, pondering, and carefully investigating the biblical teaching on forgiveness, the Holy Spirit has greatly strengthened my convictions.

Based on the biblical evidence, I am now convinced that if we forgive a brother or sister who is unrepentant, we are actually *disobedient* to the word of God. I would not have said it that way before. The option of forgiving is not open to us as followers of Christ until repentance occurs.

Forgiveness is the second component of a two-part transaction, a *response to* repentance, and therefore is inherently conditional. It cannot at the same time be both conditional *and* unconditional. We cannot have it both ways.

A sincere devotion to the Lord Jesus and a firm commitment to obeying His teaching (not to mention mere intellectual honesty) prohibits one from taking the position that it doesn't matter which of these we choose to believe. For the true followers of Jesus, there is only one option.

I am compelled by the truth of God's word to admit of no other conclusion: Any forgiveness that is doled out without the repentance of the offender is *absolutely unbiblical* and *runs contrary to the will of God!*

The verdict is unequivocal. There is not one shred of biblical support (properly interpreted) for the doctrine of unconditional forgiveness. In a court of law, it would be thrown out for lack of evidence. Sadly, many in the church are far less discerning.

The overwhelming preponderance of biblical evidence not only fails to support this doctrine, but totally annihilates it, showing it to be pure, unadulterated drivel. We must therefore reject it as the godless gruel it is, and consign it to the pit whence it came.

The proponents of this doctrine cannot furnish even one clear verse instructing, in the face of an unrepentant offender, to "forgive them anyway" (and which is forever at odds with the Lord's teaching in Matthew 18:15-17!). Conversely, I have given you several straightforward passages showing conclusively that the fundamental condition of forgiveness is *always* repentance.

If, in the face of such compelling evidence and against all truth and reason, you persist in clinging to this godless doctrine, or if you are a Christian leader who persists in making others drunk on the wine of your false teaching, then you convict yourself of hypocrisy, and demonstrate a greater love for your biases and the traditions and commandments of men than for the word of God. I pray God will open your eyes and grant you repentance leading to the knowledge of the truth, that you may escape this snare of the devil.

Our approach to Scripture is sometimes so doltish and destructive, so utterly bereft of discernment and sound reason, that it reminds me of the medieval practice of bloodletting. We gloat in our learning and pseudo knowledge, but the only thing we have done is siphon God's word of the very thing that is its essence and life.

Our biases are interpretive leeches that have bled the teaching of Scripture to the point that it is drained of its God-breathed, living truth. And then we wonder at its pallor. We marvel (the ones who dare to think and inquire honestly) that it is so devoid of vitality and power—and divinity! We revel in our anecdotes, coping strategies, and pious platitudes, but fail to see biblical results. Why? Because we have departed from biblical truth!

We have sentimentalized, psychologized, and perverted the biblical teaching of forgiveness to the point that it is no longer Christian truth. It is grave error! And this has not happened in the pub or the marketplace. It has happened right under our noses, where it can produce the most pervasive and virulent results—within our very churches and seminaries!

"Many shepherds have ruined My vineyard, they have trampled down My field; they have made My pleasant field a desolate wilderness" (Jeremiah 12:10).

If we do not repent and restore the Scriptures

to their rightful place of primacy and prominence in all that we think, say, and do—and for leaders, in all that we write, teach, and preach—then we will not survive the increasing flood of deception coming upon the church. *We* will be the cause of stumbling to many, the blood of whom God will require at our hands.

This book may be very challenging to some, perhaps most of you, but I honestly hope it has driven you to God and the truth of His word. This is my only refuge and I pray it is yours also.

I have received heated opposition to the truth expressed herein. When you expose a doctrine as deeply ingrained in the collective religious mindset as this one, that is not surprising. Whenever you strike against cherished beliefs and biases, calling into question pet doctrines, long-held traditions, and denominational prejudices, you are bound to encounter resistance.

Light exposes darkness. Truth exposes error. It cannot be otherwise. Only the truth will make you free. Thus, I have sought with all my heart and a clear conscience before God to write nothing but.

Those who love truth feel a sense of kinship with every herald of truth; those who do not, feel enmity. My goal has not been to "induce" either the one or the other, but simply to preach the truths God has burned in my heart, with a sincere desire that His Spirit bring about greater liberty, unity, and maturity in the lives of His people. In short, to build up the body of Christ; to strengthen His church.

The Lord has always raised up watchmen to sound an alarm when large segments of the church stray from the truth. Motivated by love and grave pastoral concerns, I have endeavored to thrust from your neck the heavy yoke of this false doctrine so that you may faithfully and joyfully follow the Lord Jesus, the Chief Shepherd and Guardian of your souls. And that you may cultivate ever-deepening godly relationships in the church, a rich ore of blessing far beyond words.

If you have read with an open mind and a sincere love of the truth, you may well feel a sense of joy and freedom as His truth has illumined your heart and exposed the deception of this doctrine. If not, well, I suspect you have stopped reading long before now. Or, that your heels have become deeply entrenched in the mire of unconditional forgiveness so much the more that nothing will convince you.

The Lord would call out as He taught, "He who has ears to hear, let him hear!" It is to these I write. May you hear the voice of His Spirit and follow Him into all truth, for He will lead you nowhere else.

Appendix 1

Deception Unmasked

Error never shows itself
in its naked reality,
in order not to be discovered.
On the contrary, it dresses elegantly,
so that the unwary
may be led to believe
that it is more truthful than
truth itself.

Irenaeus (c. A.D. 130–c. 200)

Many years ago I had the privilege of hearing a teaching series by the late Keith Green called, "What's Wrong with the Gospel?"[13] It was a penetrating look at some of the doctrines and ministry methods in the church. Keith said something very profound: "The greatest lie is the one closest to the truth."

I marvel at the mercy and wisdom of God. Rarely is so much truth packed into so few words.

---

13 These messages were also published in the widely circulated *Last Days Newsletter/Magazine*.

Volumes could be written expounding this. The Lord has taught me a lot about deception over the years—many painful, *hard* lessons—and I have realized (just now, in writing this) that much of it is but an elaboration of this brief statement.

The best way to counteract truth is not with a blatant lie, but to make the lie look so much like the truth that it evades detection. Deception derives its power *only* from its semblance to truth. It is never *presented* as a lie. It is poison presented as the cure.

For deception to be effective we must *believe it is the truth*. No one believes something they know is false. Its hold on us *remains* only as long as we believe it is true. That's what gives it its hook, its power. Expose it for what it is and its power is gone.

The Lord Jesus gives us a most revealing look at the character of the devil. He said the devil "does not stand in the truth, because there is *no truth in him*. Whenever he speaks a lie, he speaks *from his own nature*; for he is a liar, and *the father of* lies" (John 8:44, emphasis mine).

Another way we could say this is that he fathered all lies. He actually *invented the lie!* He spawned it. It's his creation. Every single lie in the history of the world can be traced back to him. If there is deception somewhere, it is the work of the deceiver, for deception is his calling card. Lies are his fingerprints, as it were.

Deception is no accident. It is *designed*. It is a calculated invention, a deliberate, planned falsehood made to look like truth. Deception is a strategy created by an evil spiritual mastermind whose intent is to deceive. It is a devious means employed only for that purpose. This helps us understand the origin of every false doctrine.

If someone says, "Jesus came to set the captives free," we nod in agreement, for Jesus said this at the outset of His ministry. But we tend to think only in vague generalities. Captives presuppose a captor. And a method! *Who* is holding them captive *and how?*

Paul answers this question for us. In his second letter to Timothy, he wrote, "And the Lord's bond-servant must not be quarrelsome, but be kind to all, able to teach, patient when wronged, with gentleness correcting those who are in opposition, if perhaps God may grant them repentance leading to the knowledge of the truth, and they may come to their senses and escape from the snare of the devil, having been held captive by him to do his will" (2 Timothy 2:24-26).

"The snare *of the devil*...held captive *by him.*" Okay, so we know *who* holds them. But how does he do it? The fact that Paul speaks of a snare, and that they are *held* captive is revealing. No one steps into a trap willingly or knowingly. And being held speaks of continuous present tense action. The devil is doing something that holds them captive.

"Come to their senses and escape" provides a better clue. The phrase, "come to their senses" in Greek means "to become sober again." Paul in effect is saying, "These are in a drunken stupor, a spell. They are not thinking rightly." So what breaks the spell?

Paul told Timothy to *correct* those who are in opposition (meaning they are wrong or standing in error) so that they may repent (change direction). What's the new direction? Repentance leads to *the knowledge of the truth*. Paul declares this to be the freeing agent that enables them to come to their senses and escape from the snare of the devil.

If the truth is what sets them free, then it is obvious what the snare is—*deception*. Quite simply, error *is* the snare of the devil. Deception *is* bondage. Lies do not merely bring chains. Lies *are* chains—*unseen, spiritual chains!*

The enemy can keep us in bondage only as long as he can keep us believing his lies. His power over us is to the very degree that he can *keep us* deceived. So, rather than foisting conspicuously absurd lies upon the church, he cleverly distorts and perverts the truth. He does this by counterfeiting.

No one ever tried to buy something using Monopoly money. Why? Because it looks *nothing* like real money. It's not believable. You *know* it's fake the moment you see it. The goal is to create bills that look so much like real money that it's hard to tell the difference (and then pass them off as the real thing).

Likewise, the devil must refine his lies and make them look so much like truth that the unwary embrace them and pass them on to others *as* truth. And so the contagion spreads. He has accomplished this with startling effectiveness with doctrines like unconditional forgiveness. They are taught and believed as if they are biblical truth.

God's word is alive. It has power even when misused. So, the devil quotes the word of God, like he did with Jesus (cf. Matthew 4:6), to accomplish his ends. His intent is to deceive so he takes it out of context and twists it to give false teachings an appearance of truth.

Many are deceived by the doctrine of unconditional forgiveness. By believing it and teaching it to others, the deception grows. But in the pure and searching light of God's word, we have seen it for what it is.

Thus, if you embrace the truth of the word of God, you need no longer be held captive in this snare of the enemy. Moreover, you are now equipped to help others come to their senses and also escape this snare. The only way to check the spread of this doctrine is by a passionate return to the truth. This, I pray, is the result of my work herein. Grace be with you.

Appendix 2

Consumers or Disciples?

It is the sacred duty of all
Christians . . . to be certain that their
beliefs correspond exactly to truth.

A.W. Tozer

All truth seems radical when you've left it. Truth that seems new and radical, like that presented in this book, often generates strong opinions. An opinion is simply a belief, view, or judgment formed or held about something which is not necessarily based on fact or knowledge.

If a person's opinions are founded squarely on the word of God, so that their beliefs solidify into biblical convictions, this is a good thing. If, however, opinions are held that have no basis in truth, there's a problem. Our response when confronted with truth in God's word reveals where our true loyalties lie. Those who are teachable and have a genuine love for truth reject and/or abandon opinions which conflict with the word of God. Those who are not teachable reject God's word in favor of their opinions.

The teaching in this book has liberated many from the yoke of unconditional forgiveness. I rejoice greatly and give all glory and praise to God. However, as anticipated, it has also generated opposition from those who simply refuse to see.

Thus, I felt it might be helpful to include a second appendix for the sake of those who love truth. My purpose is to respond to a few objections and to discuss some attitudes and interpretive approaches to Scripture—which dramatically affect the outcome of our exposure to truth.

Jesus made it clear in the parable of the sower that only a small minority of those who hear the word of God will have the proper heart to receive it and benefit from it. It is sobering that the Word will be unfruitful in the majority of those who hear it.

That means the truth, more often than not, will fall on deaf ears. It will produce no positive effect in the hearers. The condition of our heart impacts the quality of our hearing. Too often, this is overlooked in our study of the Bible or when we encounter biblical truth. The heart we bring to it will determine what we get out of it.

Jesus warned His disciples, "Be careful *how* you hear" (Luke 8:18). Because whoever has, more will be given; and whoever does not have, even what he thinks he has will be taken away from him. This indicates that the attitude we bring to Scripture is supremely important, and affects our ability to receive and grow in the truth.

Some of the responses to the teaching in this

book have revealed a troubling trend among those professing earnest faith in Christ. These responses have exposed an attitude which is fundamentally incompatible with genuine followers of Jesus.

Rather than displaying a firm commitment to understanding and obeying the word of God, I have observed in many what may be described as a consumeristic approach to Scripture. A consumer is one who buys goods or services for personal use. The consumer is in total control. If you're a consumer, your desire and pleasure is what steers the ship. You only buy what you want. You ignore everything else. If you don't like something, you shop around until you find what you like. Whatever is not to your liking is summarily dismissed.

While this may describe modern American culture, it should *never* describe our approach to the word of God if we are truly disciples of Jesus. Yet, this attitude seems to be increasingly commonplace in the church. Just a few examples will illustrate.

One woman said of her unbiblical opinion, "That's just what I've always believed." In other words, "Even if it's wrong, I'm not going to change. I don't care what the Bible says. I'm going to believe what I want to believe because it makes me feel good." Clearly, her comfort was paramount. Whether her belief was biblical was of secondary or no importance at all. Another said, "I don't believe it's wrong to forgive someone who doesn't repent." In other words, "I believe the specific procedure Jesus outlined is merely optional. We don't really have to follow His teaching" (cf. Matthew 28:20).

I was told of a "Bible study" where this book

was subjected to discussion to "see what they thought." Opinions shot back and forth, but there was no consensus. No final word deciding the issue. It appears the word of God is no longer the final authority in the lives of many believers. It's merely *discussed* for entertainment value. But few intend to actually obey it!

And then there was the guy, clearly rankled by the truth in this book, who tried to argue that I failed to present a compelling biblical case. I asked him to show me from Scripture where I erred. He complained that I left out an important verse (Mark 11:25).

Jesus told His disciples in this verse, "And whenever you stand praying, forgive, if you have anything against anyone; so that your Father also who is in heaven may forgive you your transgressions." In a condescending manner he urged me to "note the fact that it says nothing about repentance." Then he said triumphantly, "Jesus says plainly to forgive them."

This is a parallel passage to the Lord's teaching in Matthew 6. Consequently, I did not deem it essential to address it, considering the preponderance of the Lord's clear and expanded teaching elsewhere on the subject.

I tried to explain to him some principles about interpreting the Bible. Teaching in one place that plainly conflicts with teaching elsewhere in Scripture cannot *both* be right. The Holy Spirit does not contradict Himself. Thus, this verse in Mark must be taken in the light of other passages affording more light, where repentance is the clear prerequisite of forgiveness. But to no avail. He had apparently guzzled too much of the wine of this false teaching. It poisoned his heart and he was not able to see and think clearly.

You can't build a house on one wall. As I've said before, it's an extremely bad interpretive practice to isolate one verse and ignore the rest of what Jesus taught. We must take into account the whole of Scripture. Mark's Gospel is a brief, fast-paced account, focusing more on the actions of Jesus than His teaching. So, it's not surprising that there is only a brief mention of forgiveness in Mark. But Scripture is abundantly clear elsewhere.

In addition, Mark worked very closely with Peter (Peter refers to him as his son in his first letter, 1 Peter 5:13). The testimony of early believers is that Mark left us a written account as seen *through the eyes of Peter*. For example, the early church father, Irenaeus, said, "Mark, the disciple and interpreter of Peter handed down to us in writing the things preached by Peter."

Was Peter not there when the Lord gave very specific steps about what to do when a brother sins against us? (Matthew 18:15-17). Indeed he *was* there! Peter was the one who replied with a question about how many times he should forgive his brother. This prompted the Lord's more in depth response (Matthew 18:21-35, see chapter 1), where repentance was clearly taught as an integral part of the forgiveness process. Peter heard the Lord's teaching again in Luke 17:3, 4, where there can be absolutely no doubt that repentance must occur before forgiveness can follow. Therefore, we can only conclude that though this brother may be confused, Peter most assuredly *was not!*

Rather than accepting the unity of the Scriptures and the fact that Peter was keenly aware of the Lord's teaching about the conditional nature of forgiveness, this brother chose to pit this one verse against the clear and more complete teaching in the rest of the canon. In so doing (at least indirectly) he projects onto Peter the obtuseness and resistance to truth that he himself is guilty of.

Next, despite evidence to the contrary, he steadfastly refused to believe that the text found in Luke 23:34 was *not* an original part of Luke's Gospel (see chapter 6). This appears to be a case of burying one's head in the sand and believing what one wants to believe without regard to the accuracy or soundness of that belief.

Finally, he cited Stephen's prayer in Acts 7:60, which, he jibed, "You must have overlooked." This was the extent of his "biblical" rebuttal of the truths in this book. His unwarranted cheek I suspect only reveals some deeper conflict about which I shall not speculate. To be fair, I shall reply to this last objection before we proceed.

I did not deem this verse necessary because it seemed to me inconsequential, if not confusing to our topic. I do not believe it changes one word I've written. Stephen's prayer seems to be an example of praying for our enemies and "not loving his own life even unto death."

He had already condemned his accusers for their rebellion to God (Acts 7:51-53). And they knew it! In fact, the significance of seeing Jesus standing, rather than sitting, may poignantly underscore their condemnation. For, aside from emphasizing their blindness and wickedness in killing the Son of Man (whom Stephen vindicated by affirming that He was alive and *standing* at the right hand of God), I believe Stephen echoes a judgment from the prophet Isaiah about the Lord *removing* the rebellious leaders of His people.

> The LORD *arises* to contend, and *stands* to judge the people. The LORD enters into judgment with the elders and princes of His people, "It is you who have devoured the vineyard; the plunder of the poor is in your houses. What do you mean by crushing My people, and grinding the face of the poor?" Declares the LORD GOD of hosts (Isaiah 3:13-15, emphasis mine).

They would have known this passage and understood its significance. Alas, at this they could endure no more! Luke says they cried out with a loud voice, covered their ears, and rushed at him with one impulse (Acts 7:57).[14]

Regarding his prayer, it seems to me that Stephen was praying something along the lines of, "Lord, their wickedness is so great already, if there is any possible way, don't add this sin to the crushing weight of their guilt." We are faced here with a most convoluted question. Can one truly pray for another to be forgiven? And how does this affect personal

---

14 The significance of the Lord standing in this passage is much debated, so I offer this tentatively. If you choose not to accept it, that's fine. I'm not going to die on this hill.

responsibility before God when the Bible clearly says each will be accountable for his own deeds? (See e.g. 2 Corinthians 5:10; Ezekiel 18![15]). The general tenor of Scripture checks speculation in this direction. Therefore, to build a doctrine on this verse is supremely ill-advised.

It appears Stephen was more concerned about their eternal well-being and the state of their hearts toward *God* than with their hatred against *him* personally. His prayer is evidence that he didn't respond in hate and revenge. (As a result, his prayer is believed to be instrumental in the ensuing conversion of Saul/Paul.) I confess, I cannot see how this verse factors into our discussion.

However we understand this prayer, it cannot be used to negate the plain teaching of our Lord on forgiveness. Ultimately, Stephen's prayer and even the prayer found in Luke 23:34 (*if* it were genuine) confutes nothing I've written.

At any rate, these deal with persecution from those already condemned (John 3:36). The teaching of Jesus on forgiveness trumps the narrative portions of Scripture, and His teaching explicitly governs relationships *within the body of Christ*. As His followers, we live by a higher standard. To dispute that is to embrace folly. I asked this brother if he was willing to disregard and ignore the clear teaching of

---

15 This chapter in Ezekiel teaches personal responsibility for sin. The Lord describes three generations, and says a person will not be judged for the sins of his son or for the sins of his father, but each will be judged for his own conduct. The actions of a person cannot condemn (*or exonerate!*) another even in one's immediate family. The chapter concludes with a plea for each to repent.

Jesus in Matthew 18 and Luke 17:3, 4. No reply.

Rather than try to understand Scripture from the perspective of the whole canon, he apparently believed he was free to pick and choose what he wanted to believe and reject what didn't suit his taste. I informed him that that was not a choice left open to true followers of Jesus. We must receive the whole counsel of God.

An axiom of Protestant hermeneutics is that Scripture is its own best interpreter. One of the Reformation slogans was *Scriptura sui ipsius interpres* (Scripture interprets itself). Luther asserted, "That is the true method of interpretation, which puts Scripture alongside of Scripture in a right and proper way." Luther didn't always follow this ideal but it is nonetheless a noble objective. Wesley said, "The general rule of interpreting Scripture is this: the literal sense of every text is to be taken, if it be not contrary to some other texts; but in that case *the obscure text is to be interpreted by those which speak more plainly* (emphasis mine)."[16]

When more and brighter light is available to illumine a verse or passage, we should always readily embrace it. To hedge and remain in the shadows or to take refuge in ambiguity reveals a heart that does not love the truth. To overemphasize one brief or unclear verse that conflicts with a more complete and detailed portion of Scripture is not approaching Scripture honestly.

For example, one might rightly believe that Jesus baptized disciples, based on a reading of John

---

16 I am indebted to A. Skevington Wood for the helpful information in this paragraph.

3:22, 26; 4:1. But John gives us greater light (in 4:2) when he explains that Jesus Himself didn't baptize anyone. Therefore, to insist that He did, based on what John said previously, is to err.

This is what I earnestly tried to teach this brother. But sadly, he did not have ears to hear. It's one thing when a person honestly attempts to understand. It's quite another when, in arrogance and condescension, one takes an antagonistic and belligerent stance because they're convinced you're wrong. He simply was not teachable.

One gets a sense of the frustration Paul must have felt when he encountered the mulish cavils of the Jews (Acts 28:23-27). Some people have just enough religion to be dangerous. Armed with a thimble of truth and a bucket of pride, they become more of a blight and burden on the believing community than a boon and blessing. I suppose we have but one option in such cases (Proverbs 14:7; 23:9).

I confess I have *much* to learn! I do not yet know as I ought to know. If any can show by the plain teaching of Scripture where I err, I will quickly change my view and be the first to throw my books into the fire. But the objections addressed above are at best unconvincing.

The sincere disciple of Jesus will not approach Scripture as a consumer, to pick and choose what he wants to believe and ignore the rest. But with an honest and good heart, Jesus said, he will eagerly receive the Word, hold it fast, and bear fruit.

As devoted followers, may we never trifle with His word. Rather, let us fervently desire to grow in the knowledge of the truth, having our beliefs grounded in Scripture, that we may all speak the same thing—and "preserve the unity of the Spirit in the bond of peace." The grace and peace of our Lord Jesus Christ be with your spirit.

> These are the ones I look on with favor: those who are humble and contrite in spirit, and who tremble at My word. (Isaiah 66:2 NIV)

Made in the USA
Monee, IL
21 February 2022